WE'RE NOT
FINISHED
YET!

WE'RE NOT FINISHED YET!

PERRY & PAM STONE

We're Not Finished Yet
Mid-Life Memoirs of Perry and Pam Stone

ISBN: 0-9708611-3-3
LOC: 2005900802

Copyright 2005 by the Voice of Evangelism, Inc.
Voice of Evangelism Outreach Ministries
P.O. Box 3595
Cleveland, Tennessee, 37320
(423) 478-3456
Printed in the United States of America

Special Dedication

We see your names when we receive your letters.

We read your emails that are sent our way.

We catch a glimpse of your smiling faces when you join us at our annual conventions.

We hold your offering envelopes in our hands and ask God to return to you an eternal harvest for your obedience.

You are our partners and friends who have held our hands up during the battles and rejoiced with us in our victories. Some remember us from the early days when we couldn't afford to hire a single person—we were the only two staff members. Some have watched our children grow up, from riding tricycles at the convention center to getting a driver's license! Actually we have grown up together in the Word.

We dedicate this book to you,

Our Friends and Partners

Without your help, we could not say *We're Not Finished Yet* . . . because without you, we would never have gotten started!

CONTENTS

INTRODUCTION

We were just two young kids. I was about 20, with two years of preaching under my belt; she was 18, fresh out of high school. I was from four generations of ministers and she was from a divorced home. I was somewhat bold and outspoken; she was quiet and soft-spoken.

Two years before, I had been told that I would fail in the ministry because I did not follow the expected denominational approach to ministry. Some thought Pam would not make it as a minister's wife because she had no experience in the ministry, in traveling or in dealing with people.

Those opinions proved to be wrong!

We—Perry and Pam Stone—united and formed a ministry team whose commitment to God and His vision birthed a worldwide ministry! I was the visible voice of the ministry, but she was the unseen glue that kept it together. I have seen her at our book and tape resource table during revivals, duplicating tapes while answering a question, holding our infant son with her right arm and giving a teaching album to a friend with her left hand.

That's how it has been since 1982—Perry and Pam.

Those who know us understand that you don't talk about one without mentioning the other. Like two tomatoes on a vine, two apples growing together on the tree and two ears of corn hanging on the same stalk, Perry and Pam go together. When people see me they ask immediately, "How's Pam?" When they see Pam, their first question is, "How's Perry?"

This ministry is not a one-man solo act; it is a duet. The harmony is formed by two lives whose destinies have been woven together by time, tests, trust and triumph.

This is the story we wish to tell.

Another generation of young men and women are cutting their own trails and need knowledge from those who have traveled the road before them. Some are presently in ministry and need a faith lift. Others are partners who want to know more about the two people they love and know as Perry and Pam.

This is more than an autobiography or a story about a journey. It is the account of a blend of amazing supernatural stories and strange parallels. It shows how God wove His tapestry of purpose with simple people who used the thread of prayer. We open our hearts to reveal incidents that we have never before made public. We will detail the events that have molded the Voice of Evangelism Ministry.

After musing over numerous possible titles for this written record of events, we felt it best to simply call it the way we feel about the future—*We're Not Finished Yet.*

CHAPTER 1

ASSIGNMENT OF DEATH ON THREE GENERATIONS

And the dragon stood before the woman who was ready to give birth, to devour her Child as soon as it was born (Revelation 12:4).

ASSIGNMENT OF DEATH ON THREE GENERATIONS

The Enemy's assignment to destroy God's chosen begins early. It may be a Pharaoh in Egypt, instructing the midwives to drown the Hebrew infants in an effort to kill Moses (Exodus 1:22); or it may be an insecure Herod, demanding that Roman soldiers slay all infants less than two years of age, for fear a king of the Jews had been born (Matthew 2:16).

In my family, the strange assignments to kill, steal and destroy began many years ago.

The initial incident I will relate occurred in 1926. Nalva Dunford was a teenager in love with a young West Virginian. One evening, Nalva Dunford and her boyfriend were traveling in a Model T Ford up a winding two-lane gravel road through the West Virginia mountains, between the towns of War and Bartley.

On a sharp curve, her boyfriend lost control of the vehicle, and skidded across the road with gravel flying in all directions.

The heavy car slid over the edge of an embankment, flipped several times and landed on its side. The couple was thrown out of the car, onto the edge of a 400-foot drop-off. Nalva found herself hanging to a small tree, and saw her boyfriend holding to a bush.

Before they could scramble to safety, a large boulder that had been loosened by the accident gave way. It rolled down the hill and hit Nalva's boyfriend in the head, taking him over the side of the mountain to his death 400 feet below. With her own eyes, Nalva saw death take the one she loved. The following year she met and married Arthur Ball. The marriage produced a daughter named Ola May and a son named Morgan.

One January morning, Arthur went rabbit hunting. Late that evening, the hunting dog returned without Arthur. After four frantic days, a search party found his body in the woods near a brush pile, shot in the face. Apparently, he had tripped over a slippery log, and the gun had fired accidentally, shooting his lower jaw off. There were signs he had ripped his clothes as he lay dying.

The family wrapped Arthur's body in a blanket, and Sam Dunford made a homemade casket. With great sorrow in her heart, Nalva was left with two children and a great deal of sadness.

A CLOSE CALL

In time, Nalva met and married another young man who lived two farms away. William Stone (she called him Bill) was a farmer and a coal miner who worked hard for her and the family. Thirteen children were born to Nalva, 11 to her and William.

In those days the family lived in Johnny Cake Hollow. Their home was a small log cabin with one partition in it. Nalva became pregnant, and on February 11, 1933, a cold winter morning, she went into labor. With snow and sleet on the mountain, Bill set out to find a doctor to deliver the child. From Johnny Cake Hollow it was six miles on foot to Bradshaw. There, he learned that the doctor had gone to deliver another child at another coal camp. So Bill walked another eight miles, through a foot of snow, to Yukon, where he found Dr. Hatfield.

The two drove the doctor's Model A Ford to the bottom of Johnny Cake, where a neighbor met them with a horse. The doctor rode and William walked back up the mountain. Both men were stunned when they arrived near the house and suddenly saw a midwife running across the porch with a small bundle in a blanket. The door burst open and there was Nalva, dressed only in a cotton gown, "Bill help me . . . she has the baby . . . get her, she has the baby!"

The midwife was attempting to kidnap the six-pound baby. Bill grabbed the midwife before she could flee into the snow with the newborn. She was screaming, "This is my baby. This is my child. The Lord is giving me this baby!" In retrospect, the weather and the snow would have been too harsh for the infant, and in a matter of minutes he would have suffered severe exposure to the cold, and could have died.

1961 AUTOMOBILE ACCIDENT

More than 28 years later, that infant was a husband and the father of two children. Early one morning, he was traveling with his wife and 2-year-old son from Parsons to Buckhannon, West Virginia, in a 1961 Comet. As they topped a hill, a car with no brake lights appeared to be sitting still in the roadway.

As he attempted to pass, a pickup truck loaded with firewood appeared suddenly in the oncoming lane. In a split-second, he realized that if he passed the car, he would hit the truck head-on. On the right was a hill and a concrete abutment. His only choice was to lock the brakes, but he still hit the stalled car at 55 miles an hour.

This was before cars had seat belts and air bags. Suddenly the smell of burnt rubber and the sound of crushing metal and breaking glass shattered the peace of the highway.

Those who came upon the tragic scene wondered how many had been killed in the accident. The wife's head had struck the windshield, cutting her head and leaving a large hole in the glass. Her right knee was also injured, and her jaw was broken.

The tremendous impact was so forceful that the driver's hands bent the steering wheel. The wreck ruptured the wall of his stomach and shattered the tissue lining in his throat.

When the injured parents regained consciousness, they realized in a panic that their two-year-old son was missing. They found him lying under the metal dashboard, amid broken glass. Blood was on his forehead. In shock and in pain herself, the mother reached over and picked up her son, believing he had been killed by the awful impact of the crash.

Moments before, the young fellow had been playfully standing in the front seat, between his mom and dad. Just five minutes before the accident, the driver had said to his wife, "Sit him down. If we have an accident he could go through the windshield." His words were prophetic; but instead of the windshield, the little boy hit the hard metal dashboard.

Both parents believed, initially, that the impact had broken the boy's neck. Suddenly, the child began to move. Then he began to cry the greatest cry a parent could hear! As the injured parents reached out for the baby, he started saying, "My shoe, my shoe!"

Friends had bought the little fellow a new pair of shoes a few days before, and the impact of the accident had knocked one of them off of his foot. The mother recalls:

> I was in shock at the time, and when I picked up my son, someone was opening my door telling me to get out of the car in case it caught fire. I was able to get

out, but I was still in shock and in severe pain. Someone drove us to the emergency room.

Thankfully, the child survived the car wreck. His aunt picked glass out of his hair for several days, while his mother recovered from surgery and the father healed from his own cuts and bruises.

NOW THE REST OF THE STORY

As radio news commentator Paul Harvey says, "Now the rest of the story. . . ."

♦ Nalva Stone, the young woman who lost her boyfriend in a sudden wreck, experienced the early sorrow of a husband's tragic death and almost had her newborn kidnaped by a midwife, was my grandmother—my father's mother.

♦ The infant the midwife attempted to kidnap was my father, the Reverend Fred Stone.

♦ I was the little boy in the car accident!

Three generations of our family had heart-stopping brushes with death: Nalva, my grandmother, Fred, my father, and I. Satan was trying to stop something God wanted to go forward.

I grew up hearing the story of the 1961 car accident. As a young boy, Mom showed me the pictures of the car and related the story many times. My father has frequently recounted publicly how, minutes before the impact, a large deer came out of nowhere and blocked the road. Dad impatiently, but gently, tapped the deer with the car attempting to get it out of the road. Had he waited about one minute we could have avoided the accident.

A few years ago, Dad shared with me the story of his mother's accident and his near kidnaping by the midwife. As we discussed these strange matters, I asked Dad, "Looking back on these three incidents, what would have happened had your mother married Arthur instead of your father, Bill? What would have happened if the midwife had been successful, and you had died while she trudged through the snow?"

What about the car accident? If any one of these attacks from Satan had been successful, there would never have been a world-wide ministry called The Voice of Evangelism, reaching millions of souls each year with the gospel!

HOW MUCH DOES THE ENEMY KNOW?

Both Dad and I agree that the Adversary cannot determine a believer's future. He can initiate an attack, but he cannot determine the final outcome.

♦ Jesus was crucified, but Satan did not foresee the Resurrection.

♦ Satan saw Peter deny the Lord, but he was unaware of the impact and potential of the coming Day of Pentecost.

♦ Paul and Silas were imprisoned, but the enemy did not foresee the jailer and his household being saved.

♦ Paul was shipwrecked, but the Enemy didn't see that an entire island would be converted to Christ through Paul's ministry!

♦ The Enemy knew John was a political prisoner on the Island of Patmos, but he was unaware of God's plan to reveal to John the vision in the Book of Revelation.

Look at the ministry of Christ.

1. As a child the Roman soldiers came after Him, but He escaped into Egypt (Matthew 2:13).

2. After his first public sermon the crowd attempted to throw Him off a cliff at Nazareth, but He walked through the midst of them and was supernaturally protected (Luke 4:29-30).

3. Once a storm almost sank the ship on which He was a passenger, but the entire crew and Christ survived (Mark 4:37-41).

4. In Jerusalem they attempted to stone him with stones, but

could not because his "hour had not yet come" (John 7:30). God's destiny is greater than Satan's death traps. God's sovereignty will always prevail against Satan's strategies. God's purpose will overcome Satan's power. If you have a pre-ordained assignment from God, then the Enemy will try to stop it early in your life.

To be triumphant in the faith, you must make wise choices and watch as well as pray. As long as you are breathing, you can say, "I am not finished yet!"

LESSONS I HAVE LEARNED IN THESE EXPERIENCES

- ♦ Attacks from the Enemy and assignments of evil can be formed years before a person's birth.

- ♦ An attack does not signify a defeat; it is simply a delay in the process of victory.

- ♦ God always has a way of escape planned, even before the attack comes.

- ♦ The Enemy may plan and implement the assault, but he cannot determine the outcome!

CHAPTER 2

THE LEGACY CONTINUES

When I call to remembrance the genuine faith that is in you, which dwelt first in your grandmother Lois and your mother Eunice, and I am persuaded is in you also (2 Timothy 1:5).

THE LEGACY
CONTINUES

My family has been blessed by God with a very rich heritage. In the past four generations, there have been more than 179 total years of ministry in my family lineage.

- ♦ Grandmother Bava's uncle, Robert L. Rexrode, was in full-time ministry for over 30 years.

- ♦ John Bava, my mother's father, preached the gospel for 67 years.

- ♦ My father, Fred Stone, has been in full-time ministry for 54 years.

- ♦ At the time of this writing, I have been in full-time ministry for more than 28 years.

When four consecutive generations are involved in the same sport, work or politics, it is considered a legacy. Claude Bowers, the founder of Christian Channel 55 in Orlando, Florida, has often told his viewers that "Perry Stone is a fourth-generation minister, and that means he has a legacy of ministry in his heritage." This legacy began during one of the toughest seasons in American history, the Great Depression.

THE TERRIBLE GREAT DEPRESSION

Both Robert L. Rexrode and my Grandfather, John Bava, began their preaching ministries during the time of the Great Depression. This was a most difficult time for 20th century America, since unemployment was as high as 30 percent in some cities. Jobs were scarce or nonexistent, and anyone in full-time ministry, especially a traveling ministry, risked near starvation for the family during the icy winter months.

John Bava once told of receiving an offering of one nickel in a revival he was preaching. Yet, the zeal and spiritual fire that burned in the souls of these poor "mountain Christians" sustained them through the toughest of times.

To trace the legacy of this ministry, we begin in the late 1920's, in the mountains of West Virginia. In those days, most men who could find a job worked in the lumber yards or the coal mines. Years later, coal would be removed by machines; but in those days, the black sweat of a coal miner, a pick, a shovel and mining mules were used to bring the coal from the belly of the earth to be sold in the marketplace.

Coal camps were quite common in West Virginia. The camps were small communities that were built near the mines where the miners and their families lived. Each camp had its own store. During the Depression, the government issued special stamps for certain food purchases, and rationed sugar and other commodities.

This was before birth control was common, and many miners had large families with as many as 5 to 15 children. In this setting, our ministry legacy begins.

A PENTECOSTAL PIONEER

Before being converted to Christ and called into the ministry, Robert L. Rexrode worked with the Secret Service Department of the U.S. Government. By the time he had finished his duties with the Secret Service, he had made an enemy, and decided to kill him with a gun. The plot was exposed, however, and he was forced from his home.

The heavy mental load he carried began wearing him down. He contracted influenza, and his health began to deteriorate rapidly. His sickness and his concern for the condition of his soul led him to make contact with Christians, which eventually brought him to a decision to follow Christ.

He received the Lord as his personal Savior. Supplementing his income as a barber, Robert began preaching in the Brethren and the Methodist churches. In 1934, he confessed: "I would preach, use tobacco, use vulgar language and drink whiskey. Friends, I was not the only preacher who did that, and some are still doing that. . . ."

Robert's sickness became so severe that 13 physicians and two hospitals gave him up to die. In desperation, he began to seek more of God's Presence for his life. Eventually, he attended an open air meeting in the park in Elkins, West Virginia. There, he listened to a minister preach a "strange doctrine about the Holy Spirit's power and speaking with other tongues."

During the altar service, one woman fell to the ground, shaking and "praying in tongues." Conviction smote him until he, too, was baptized in the Spirit. He sought for God to sanctify him from his many unclean habits. One day, after intense prayer, he was instantly healed and totally restored to health after twelve years of continual sickness.

During the Great Depression, R. L. began ministering the Word of God, often to small congregations of 10 to 20 people. The times were difficult and he and his family lived at the poverty level.

In a small pamphlet titled *Testimony of R. L. Rexrode*, he personally wrote:

> We have had to suffer much. . . . In one revival . . . our provisions were cut off from us. This was in the wintertime, and on account of my car being broke we could not get away. One day we had a small dish of gravy made from milk of cows that had eaten wild onions. [This was] divided between the six of us. The next day we had nothing at all to eat, yet the presence of the Lord was with us. . . .

He also wrote of another difficult time:

> More than once I have said to my wife, "We had better give up preaching for a while," because her feet would be on the ground and our clothes would be in such a shape that we were not fit to appear in public. With tears in her eyes, she would say, "Bob, let's try it a while longer."

> I distinctly remember one time when her toes were sticking out of her shoes, and I had half–soled my shoes with inner tubes. . . .

He concluded his pamphlet with these words:

> At the time of this writing, November 15, 1934, I am 273 miles from home. I have just received a letter from my wife, telling me that she and the babies are in need. I am doing all I can. . . .

Those days were lonely and difficult days for many ministers who received and preached the message of Pentecost, or the Baptism in the Holy Ghost. Most of the townsfolk who were religious attended older mainline churches. In some areas, such as the northeast, the prominent religion was Catholicism.

Pentecostals were considered by many to be a strange cult, or a fanatical fringe group. Some people even called them religious nuts. Their meetings were often disrupted by mockers and scoffers. When a person received the gift of the Holy Ghost, they were usually ostracized, and at times physically attacked by unbelievers. Robert not only continued to preach in his unique way, but he also organized a gospel band that began attracting sinners to his meetings.

SALVATION AT THE SCHOOL HOUSE

In September 1929, Rev. Rexrode was conducting a revival at the Methodist School House in Pierce, West Virginia. One thing that drew people to the services was the bluegrass gospel music he featured each night. His traveling band was called the Rexrode Happy Band.

In those days there were no "protracted meetings." Instead, traveling evangelists would go to a city or town and stay until revival broke out and souls were being saved. Among the large crowds Bro. Rexrode's meeting attracted were two brothers, John and Joe Bava.

Both were sons of an Italian immigrant who had come to America from Calabria, Italy, around the turn of the century. John saw the colorful poster announcing the Rexrode revival, and began attending because he enjoyed the music.

Eventually, the seed of the gospel penetrated the hearts of both Joe and John, who went to the altar and received salvation. They prayed so loudly that those living several blocks from the meeting could hear them praying.

There was a difference in the preaching of R.L. Rexrode and other ministers. Joe and John knew it was the Holy Spirit Baptism which he boldly preached. Soon, they also began to seek this "Pentecostal experience."

One night, John received the infilling of the Spirit. Returning home to his Italian-Catholic father, John was still speaking in other tongues. In the 1960s John wrote in his booklet, *My Life Story*:

My father and mother had gone to bed. Hearing my uninhibited tongues-speaking, they promptly came downstairs. When Dad looked at me, I saw both his hands quivering at his side. I knew he was scared, for we could not talk in Italian and had never spoken in a foreign language before. Finally, he and mother went to bed and Joe walked his girlfriend home.

About an hour later I heard my brother coming up the walk. He was singing and praising God in an unknown language. About that time I heard my father's feet hit the floor, as he shouted, "I'm going downtown and have that preacher arrested for making my boys go crazy."

By this time I knew dad was really angry . . . and scared, too. When Joe had taken his girlfriend home, they had knelt down and prayed for the baptism and had received it right there.

CONVERSION OF AN ITALIAN CATHOLIC

Pete Bava, John's father, was a heavy drinker and had no concern for spiritual matters. He rejected John and Joe's religion as fanaticism. John had a heavy burden for his father.

During the winter, Pete came down with a severe illness. He began missing work in the mines, and eventually became paralyzed in his arms and legs. A doctor's report was bleak; Pete's condition was critical. He said that Pete could not live much longer. John and Joe asked a minister, Rev. J. M. Kile, to come and pray for him.

By now, most of Pete's friends thought he was going to die. Seven of his drinking buddies came over and were discussing how sad they were that Pete would be shortly departing this life. Pete was so weak he could hardly whisper. At 11 o'clock the following morning, two ministers came to the house and told Pete that "God has power to raise you up . . . if you will serve Him." Pete agreed for the ministers to pray.

The energetic prayers continued for some time. Rev. Kile said, "Pete, move your legs." Pete instantly began moving his legs. John wrote:

> When we saw his legs move, it seemed like the room suddenly filled with the great power of God. We all arose from our knees and began to praise God. The next instant, it seemed as though an unseen force hit Dad. He threw up his arms, rose up in the bed and bounced to the floor, shouting and praising God!

Pete was instantly healed! His seven drinking buddies all died before he did, and Pete lived to be over 93 years of age! He never missed a church service, and loved to tell about his conversion and healing. He always wore a black suit, a black hat and black leather shoes. His favorite story was his own personal testimony, which he told in broken English with a strong Italian accent.

JOHN AND LUCY BAVA

Robert Rexrode and his wife, Lillian, had three children. They also raised their neice, a young Italian girl whose father had immigrated to America but returned to Italy after his wife's death. He never came back to America, and this left his young daughter to be raised by his wife's sister. She happened to be the wife of R. L. Rexrode.

The girl, Lucille Luprese (Lucy), was young and attractive. She played the guitar and mandolin for the Rexrode Band. During a school house revival, John felt an attraction to Lucy and after some time, they both fell in love. They wanted to get married, but Robert objected, knowing it would break up the band. John and Lucy chose to elope on February 8, 1935. John said:

> When he found out what I did, he could have run me out of town. Eventually, he got over it!

Singing, Songwriting and the Music Industry

Although John only had an 11th grade education and worked in the mines, as most young men in that area did, he became a prolific poet and songwriter. When he got home from the mines, he would spend his time writing poems and songs. John was also a talented singer and gifted accordion player. Lucy was a noted guitarist who played a Martin guitar John purchased for her. The couple traveled to churches, homecomings and public events to sing their songs and minister to souls.

John became so consumed with the music ministry and songwriting that he took a chicken coop behind his house and turned it into a print shop. He began printing a magazine called *Musical Echoes*. It was sent to radio stations and station managers across the nation. In a short time the magazine had a subscription of 1,000 people in America and Canada. John worked in the mines during the day, in the evenings he spent long hours in the print shop.

Soon, John found himself getting only about three hours of sleep a night. His mailbox was inundated with requests for *Musical Echoes*, as letters began to pour in from throughout the nation. These included letters from celebrities such as Tennessee Ernie Ford, Brenda Lee and Lawrence Welk. The famous country music star, Gene Autry, was also a reader of John's magazine.

By now he had written numerous songs, so he formed two music publishing companies, Panhandle Music and John Bava's Music. He also formed his own record label called Cozy Records, and pressed records for literally hundreds of singers in the country, hillbilly and gospel music fields. His songs were sung on radio programs and stations throughout the nation in the early years. Later, they were heard on national television programs such as Hee Haw.

During the latter part of John's life, noted country-western singer Ricky Van Shelton recorded the song, "Don't Overlook Salvation," one of the oldest gospel songs John had written. Ricky said it had been his parent's favorite gospel song!

John's printing business ceased when the chicken coop housing his printing machines burned to the ground. He and Lucy also became the proud parents of two girls, Juanita, born in 1935, and Janet, born in 1937. Both girls were musicians and singers as teenagers, and eventually the entire family team sang together as the Bava Family Singers. During he 1950s, their voices were heard on radio stations throughout northern West Virginia.

Meanwhile, on the opposite end of the state, God was preparing a young man for his own destiny in ministry, and for a special, life-long connection to the Bava family.

REVIVAL ON THE OTHER END OF THE STATE

The southern half of West Virginia was known as the coal fields. One family living in the hollows near Bartley, West Virginia, was the Stone clan. A coal miner, William Stone was raising 11 children, including a son named Fred.

Freddy, as he was affectionately called, was the third child, all of whom grew up in the difficult culture of the coal fields. Fred attended Big Creek High School in War, West Virginia. This is the home of the famous "rocket boys," a story told in the movie *October Sky.*

In the late 1940s, the coal mines were booming. Communities were divided into coal camps. These camps often spawned drunkenness, fornication and fighting. Few men were religious, and for a man to become a Christian meant he would be labeled a "sissy." It was unheard of to see grown men cry or express public emotion. Only a spiritual revival could change the moral degeneration and spiritual depression that gripped these camps.

In this spiritual and cultural setting, a handful of Christians became overwhelmed with a burden to see a revival. Three women and three elderly ministers began a nightly prayer meeting, going from house to house. Continuously, they bombarded heaven, asking God to visit the coal camp with a true revival. After six months, Mildred Collins, a young female evangelist, felt impressed to begin a revival.

The services started at the Church of God in Christ, in a tiny "shotgun-style" church in Flattop. The church was nestled in a small valley between two rugged West Virginia mountains. The impact of this revival was felt throughout the entire region. Through prayer and preaching, the revival continued nightly for three and one half years—in the Flattop and Yukon Churches of God in Christ.

Popularly known as the "Appalachian Coal Field Revival," the revival's final results counted 300 individuals who were converted and over 300 who were filled with the Holy Spirit. A remarkable feature was that 70 young men and four women who were converted to Christ also accepted the call into the ministry during this 42-month outpouring.

One November night, a 17-year-old coal miner's son, Fred, was invited by his half brother, Morgan, to hear Mildred Collins preach. Sitting on the back row, Fred said he heard Mildred call his name, saying, "Fred, if you should die at midnight tonight, where would you be in eternity?" Fred claimed she said this twice, although Mildred later said she did not make the statement . . . and she didn't even know Fred Stone or his name! Fred calls it a "supernatural manifestation of the Holy Spirit!"

Conviction pulled on his heart and drew him like a magnet to the altar. That night, a skinny, black-haired coal miner's son was brought into the kingdom of God and a course was charted that would prove to be a remarkable journey.

During the revival, three young men became close friends and prayer partners. They were Fred Stone, Lloyd Addair and Chester Hurst. They were vibrant youths on fire for God! Throughout the next year, other revivalists occasionally pitched their tents or conducted revival crusades in the larger communities. One such noted evangelist was Thea F. Jones. From his teens, Rev. Jones was recognized as a remarkable preacher. Fred said he had never heard anyone who could preach a gospel message like Thea Jones. He often quoted up to 300 scriptures in one service. Yet, it was the prayer lines where the sick were prayed for that seized the attention of those attending the meeting. Fred recalls:

> During Thea's meeting, I saw tangible physical miracles happen before my eyes. On one occasion, a woman with a goiter as large as a baseball hanging from her neck, stood before Thea. He touched the goiter on both sides and yelled, "You foul-choking spirit, I command you in the name of Jesus Christ to be loosed from this woman. Let her go in Jesus' name!"
>
> He then commanded the woman to "Swallow in Jesus' name!" As the woman swallowed, the goiter instantly vanished from her neck. At that moment, the power of God struck the place and people began to weep and run to the front for prayer!

This tent campaign birthed a spiritual hunger in the lives of the three young men to see God's power demonstrated in their own lives. Fred built a small, one-room, eight-by-ten-foot cabin in the mountains to use for prayer and Bible study. Another close friend of Fred's was a young man in his late 20s named Al Collins.

Al was suddenly stricken with cancer in his brain and lungs, and died suddenly. Many questioned why the Lord allowed him to die at such an early age, especially when the saints were praying for his healing and he had felt called to preach. Somewhat discouraged, Fred began to seek God about his future. He had a meeting scheduled with the local draft board.

A SUPERNATURAL CALL FROM GOD

In the fall of 1950, the Korean War was raging and young men from West Virginia were being drafted. Fred received a notice from the draft board. Feeling burdened, he hiked up the mountain to the cabin to be alone and pray. He was heavy-hearted and needed to hear from the Lord. Moving his chair outside the cabin, he leaned it near the side of the door and began reading the Bible. A simple prayer time turned into hours of intercession.

Suddenly he heard footsteps at the corner of the small cabin. As he leaned over to see what was happening, he felt the hand of a person touch his head. Instantly, he slumped over, thinking he was having a heart attack. Suddenly he felt he was out of his body. Fred relates what happened:

> There I was, slumped over in that chair, with my head on the Bible. I thought I was dead, yet, there was no fear. I had perfect peace. In an instant, I felt my soul (it may have been my spirit) being whisked, it seemed, as fast as the speed of light. In a few moments the feeling of traveling through space stopped and I was standing in the midst of the most beautiful blue atmosphere I had ever seen.
>
> In the far distance I saw a round, silver light. It began moving swiftly toward me. As it came closer, the silver color changed and I saw Al Collins, who had passed away a few weeks before. I lifted my hand to greet him, and he raised his hand and said, "Freddy, God sent me to tell you that you must preach." He lowered his hand and turned as if to leave. Suddenly, he raised his hand again, and announced, "Freddy, God said you must preach." In an instant he stepped back into the ball of silver light, and was gone.
>
> I was carried backward, in a fast-moving fashion, and in an instant I could see my body slumped in the chair about 50 feet away. The Lord slipped my soul (or spirit) back into my body like a glove fitting over a hand. Instantly, I sat up in the chair. When I entered into my physical body, the hair on my arms and neck was stand-

ing straight up. I wept and continued to pray for some time.

More than 54 years after this experience, Fred still cannot relate it to anyone without tears coming to his eyes. A few weeks later, at the meeting with the draft board, Fred shared his desire to minister with those present, but said he would serve his country as a medic or a chaplain's assistant if he was needed.

The Board had him step out of the room while they made a decision, which they announced: "Mr. Stone, we believe you can best serve our country as a minister here in the United States. We will keep you informed if we should need you." The draft board never called and soon Fred began ministering throughout the area.

With no automobile for transportation, Fred often packed his suitcase and hitchhiked from town to town. A few times he managed to scrape up enough money for a bus ride to the revival. Many times the call of God sustained him when the finances did not. Often, he shared what he received in offerings with his parents who were in financial need. Because Fred spent substantial time in fasting and prayer, remarkable miracles began to follow his ministry. Fred became very sensitive to the spirit world as illustrated in the story of his youngest brother, Kenny Edgar.

ENCOUNTERING SPIRITS OF INFIRMITY

In the early 1950's, another son was born to the family of William and Nalva Stone. They named him Kenny Edgar. Physically he looked healthy but as time passed, the family noticed he was unable to walk or sit up. Extensive medical examinations, including x-rays, indicated there was nothing visibly wrong to cause this infirmity.

During this same time, the child would let out screams and double over in pain, which appeared to come from his chest area. At this time Fred was traveling and ministering, returning home occasionally between meetings. Nalva noticed that when Fred was present and holding the child, little Kenny demonstrated no signs of pain in his body. He would rest peacefully in Fred's arms.

One evening Fred took the crying child from his mother and dad's room and took him to a little bunk bed where he was sleeping, holding Kenny on his chest. He would gently stroke the little boy's back and quietly pray for him. After some time, Fred saw a colorful vision. He saw a creature with distorted features and teeth, and dull, gray skin. The creature stood at the foot of the bed, and suddenly thrust its hand into the chest area, near the heart of the child, twisting its hand. Instantly the infant began to jerk its body and scream in pain.

Fred rose up in bed, grabbing the child with his right arm and shoving his left hand out toward the creature. He lunged toward it and yelled out, "You foul spirit, I command you to get your hands off this child in Jesus name." The creature had a look of terror and stepped back about five feet. It replied to Fred, "I cannot do anything to this child while you are here, but you will be gone in three days and there is no one else like you in this house and when you are gone I will do what I want to." The creature evaporated from his sight.

Fred grasped Kenny tight and continued praying for some time. Later that night the Lord gave him a spiritual dream. He recalls:

> In this dream, I saw little Kenny lying in bed between Mom and Dad. From the waist up, Mom and Dad looked like humans; but from the waist down, they looked like swine. I knew that in the Bible a swine represented a spiritual backslider (2 Peter 2:22).

> The Lord spoke to me and said, "You must tell your mother and father that I have given them this child for a blessing to them when they get old (Kenny was the youngest of 12 children). If they will serve Me, I will heal him; if not, I will take him on. I want this child raised to follow me."

The next day I told Mom and Dad the dream. Dad cursed and said, "Why would God take him when we decide how we want to live and Kenny doesn't?" I answered, "Dad, you will live to be old (he lived to be 84), and Kenny will help take care of you. But God doesn't want him raised in a life of sin, and you and Mom aren't serving God."

At that time, Mother and Dad did not repent and serve God. Thirty days later, I received a call where I was preaching a revival that Kenny Edgar had died. Both of my parents were grieved, but months later they received Christ in one of my revivals!

The revelations in this story are amazing.

♦ First, God gives us children to care for us as we get older.

♦ Secondly, God can take a child when it is young if He sees the child is going to be raised in sin or the parents are currently living in sin.

♦ Thirdly, God's healing and deliverance may be tied to the spiritual obedience of the parents. The child needed deliverance, but at that time the personal sins in the home kept the door open to spiritual attack.

Strange and supernatural experiences became common as Fred spent days in fasting and prayer. On one occasion he and his friend, Lloyd Addair, were knocking on doors, inviting people to church. In one home they were asked to pray for a woman with a cancer that had eaten into her face, exposing the white bone in her cheek. They anointed her with oil and prayed the prayer of faith. Several days later, it was discovered that God had healed the woman of cancer. New skin was already covering her face!

REVIVAL RESULTS INCLUDE A GOOD WIFE

One thing is certain: A good revival can produce a good wife! As God's destiny would have it, Fred Stone was invited to preach a revival at the Church of God in Fairmont, West Virginia. The Bava family attended the Fairmont church. During this revival, Fred met Juanita, the beautiful dark-haired daughter of John and Lucy Bava.

With his wavy jet-black hair, Fred was so handsome that Juanita thought he looked like a Hollywood movie star. Juanita was as cute as a teddy bear, and the young couple hit it off almost immediately. After dating and getting to know each other for about a year, the couple was married in Fairmont, West Virginia, on Saturday, July 9, 1955.

How God wove the lives of these families together reads almost like a detailed movie script. Pete Bava came to America and had two daughters and two sons. One son, John, met Lucy Rexrode during a revival where he received Christ. John married Lucy and they had two daughters, Janet and Juanita.

Meanwhile, Fred Stone was converted, called into the ministry, and met Juanita Bava. They fell in love and were married. This union produced four children: Diana Ruth, Perry, Phillip Eugene and Melanie Dawn. Their second child was named Perry Fred Stone, Jr., after his father. Thus, after 80 years, God has brought us into a legacy of ministry.

Without question, the two people who had the greatest impact on my life and ministry were Granddad Bava and my Father, Fred. During my childhood, and into my early teens I learned many ministry concepts from my grandfather.

What I Learned from Granddad Bava

When I was a preteen, Grandfather had a small recording studio in his house. As a child I would sneak into the room and put on a reel-to-reel tape, recording my voice on the magnetic ribbon.

Once, I accidentally erased one of Granddad's radio programs. When I got into his stuff, he would threaten to whip me "West

Virginia style." This meant he would use a miner's belt; and that belt looked like a hangman's noose to a kid my age!

Every Christmas except one, Pam and I went to Grandma and Granddad's house in Davis, West Virginia. The little town of about 600 people is the highest town east of the Rocky Mountains. In the winter, it snows there when it doesn't snow anywhere else in the entire state. Pam always enjoyed Christmas at Grandpa and Grandma's house!

Pam remembers what I told her before we were married:

> Before we were married, Perry made it clear that as long as Grandma and Grandpa Bava were living, we would spend Christmas at their house. The only one we missed was the year Jonathan was born on December 23. After driving 10 hours and arriving late at night, we always knew they would always be up waiting for us, with Granddad in his pajamas and Grandma in her housecoat. The first thing Grandma would say was, "Are you hungry?" Perry would chow down on her homemade vegetable soup.
>
> Granddad liked several board games. One was Scrabble and the other was called Acquire, a real estate game. The competition would become so intense that Perry would have to stand up and walk around, especially if he was losing. Granddad was hard to beat at either game, and had a sharp mind, even into his early 80s.
>
> Grandmother loved to cook, and she spent the entire day before Christmas in the kitchen. On Christmas day, the little three-bedroom house would have as many as 25 people in it, listening to the Christmas story, praying and exchanging gifts.
>
> Another tradition was the Western Steer restaurant in Elkins. Grandma and Granddad traveled to this steak house, 35 miles away, every day to eat. It was like a religious tradition. The restaurant even put a plaque on the wall calling John Bava their most loyal customer!

Under no condition would Granddad miss church on Sunday. Even with a foot of snow on the ground, he would still go to church at age 82. If the weather was too bad to get out, he would call the pastor and ask him to pick up his tithes. This is why he was so blessed throughout his life.

Pam and I want to have a home and marriage similar to my grandparents. They were married for over 65 years before Granddad passed away. Months before he died, he dreamed he saw his little brother, Tony, and his mom and dad standing on a hill, saying, "Johnny, it's time for you to come home." Twice he dreamed of seeing a large, beautiful home in heaven. He knew God was preparing to take him home.

I was in Africa when Pam called and said, "Granddad had emergency surgery, but can't wake up." After his surgery, three strokes injured his brain and left him unable to speak or say a final goodbye. I left a major meeting in Africa early to return home and stand beside the bed of my dear friend, Granddad Bava.

Arriving late at night, I walked into the intensive care unit of the hospital and saw him lying there, connected to various medical paraphenalia. Touching his hand, I remembered a dream he had that impacted him for many years. One of his dear church members, Bill Fishel, had passed away. Granddad was saddened because he had buried over 50 of his close friends while pastoring the Gorman Church of God. After Bill's death, he retired from pastoring at age 77.

Just after Bill died, Granddad had a wonderful dream. He saw numerous men from his church who had passed away over the many years. He saw Freddie Otto and his own father, Pete Bava, gathered together as though waiting for someone. They were standing in front of a large, white gate. Suddenly, the gate swung open and Bill Fishel ran toward the men. They all began to jump, shout and worship God, smiling and hugging one another. Granddad told me this, years ago, with tears in his eyes.

Standing at his deathbed, I knew that in a few days those 50 souls would be standing at a gate and welcoming the soul and spirit of their beloved pastor and friend, John Bava. Two days later, on April 11th, 1997, He passed away. He entered the beautiful white gate that he saw in a dream many years before!

Grandma was so lonely without him and wanted to be with him. She lived longer than Granddad, and spent time with us in Cleveland. She came to the office, stuffed letters, and helped in little things in the ministry. I would say, "Can I pay you something, Granny?" She would smile big and say, "No. I'm just working for my crown!" Despite her loneliness, her mind remained clear and sharp, and her smile never ceased until October 24, 2002, the day of her departure.

GRANDMOTHER'S LAST DREAM

I saw her just before she passed away in a Cleveland hospital. In our last conversation, I leaned over her bed and she told me the dream she had.

> I dreamed I saw your grandfather in heaven, dressed in unusual clothing—like the work clothes he would wear when he was working on a house or an apartment (he was a great carpenter). He said, "Lucy you've got to come and see this. We have been working hard to get things ready. You must come and see this."
>
> He motioned to me and I began climbing up a hill. At the top, I looked down and saw the largest banquet hall I had ever seen. There were tables draped in the most beautiful white, glowing linen as far as my eyes could see.
>
> People were coming through huge back doors to find their places. Your grandfather said, "Lucy, this is where we will have the Marriage Supper of the Lamb. Our

table is right over there." He pointed to the center of the huge room. "It's almost ready" he said. "We are all working hard to get things ready!"

Grandmother seldom had dreams, so I knew she had experienced a true revelation from the Lord. This lovely saint passed away a few days later. She went to meet the two men she loved more than life, Jesus and Granddad.

After many years of ministry I can see clearly the important things my grandfather taught me.

♦ He taught me the importance of the printed page.

♦ He inspired me to use recordings to spread the message.

♦ He taught me the importance of music, and the value of writing gospel music.

♦ He showed me that life can be joyous and serious at the same time.

♦ He never argued with grandmother; he taught me the value of being a loving companion.

♦ He never spoke negatively about people. He taught me to look for the best in a person.

Several of his gifts are evident in my own life. One such gift is songwriting and publishing. My very first song was written in Bulgaria in the early 1990s. *Close to the Cross but Far from the Blood* was recorded by the McKameys. My two most noted songs are *Fire, Fire, Fire*, recorded by more than 15 different individuals and groups, and the song, *Let the Veil Down*, recorded in 2004 by Judy Jacobs.

LEARNING FROM DAD

Young people love hearing interesting stories. Growing up, I did not always pay attention when Dad would preach. Many times I remember him pointing his right hand toward heaven and, at the same time, snapping the fingers of his left hand at me on the front row because I was talking or not paying attention. If he snapped twice in one service, it meant I would see "stars and stripes"—I saw the stars and he laid on the stripes!

But once Dad began to tell one of those amazing stories, I sat up and listened. From my early teens I saw firsthand many of the gifts of the Holy Spirit operate in his life. He had a keen gift of seeing the unseen, especially in the area of sin. Through the Holy Spirit he knew when his sheep (members) were secretly sinning. He would call them up and tell them what they were doing, where they were doing it, and who was involved.

At times the person would almost pass out in fear, or would accuse Dad of spying on him. In reality, the "spy" was the Holy Spirit! It was difficult for any of us four kids to sin when we were growing up. Not that we wanted to, but we knew if we did the Lord would show Dad and we would be "up a creek." Certainly, his prayers protected Diana, Phillip, Melanie and me.

Dad's gifts and my gifts are the same in many ways. Yet, they are different in other ways. Our preaching styles are the same in many ways, but our content and methods differ. He has a strong compassion for the sick, and miracles occur when he prays. I do too, but I have an especially strong burden to see men and women baptized in the Holy Spirit. Since 1977, I have seen 35,000 individuals from at least eight denominations baptized in the Holy Ghost with the evidence of speaking with other tongues. On the other hand, since 1995, Dad has seen over 15 people healed of various forms of cancer.

In our main meetings, Dad often prays for the sick and I minister to those who desire the infilling of the Spirit. In Acts 8, Philip preached in Samaria and souls were converted and delivered from evil spirits. When the time came for the believers to receive the Holy Spirit, they sent Peter and John to lay hands on them to receive the gift of the Holy Spirit.

Each apostle had a particular gift. Some planted, some watered and God gave the increase. One of the mistakes a pastor can make is to bring someone on his staff who has the same type of gifts he has just to complement him. A successful pastor will bring in ministers who operate in various gifts and offices, in order to balance out the needs of the church.

Dad is one of the greatest men of prayer I have ever known. He once told me that when he passes away, he wants me to tell the folks at his funeral that he maintained his integrity as a minister and he only loved one woman all of his life—his wife and the mother of his children. His simple and humble lifestyle has inspired many, and I have learned many valuable lessons from him.

LESSONS I HAVE LEARNED IN THESE EXPERIENCES

+ I have learned how to pray, and I have learned the value of prayer.

+ I have learned how the gifts of the Spirit operate and minister to people.

+ I have learned that one must remain humble and simple in faith to be used of God.

+ I have learned the importance of integrity and keeping a good name.

+ I have learned that anything is possible if a person can have faith and believe.

Today, I am glad to say the legacy of ministry continues. I'm still running and I'm not finished yet!

CHAPTER 3

ONLY IN A PREACHER'S HOME

I urge you, brethren . . . know the housefold of Stephanas, that . . . they have devoted themselves to the ministry of the saints (1 Corinthians 16:15).

ONLY IN A PREACHER'S HOME

My earliest memories of growing up in a "preacher's home" are of when I was about four years old and we moved to Big Stone Gap, Virginia. The beautiful community nestled like an egg in a nest in the mountains of southwest Virginia. The minister's house, called a parsonage, was a white cinder-block building, with two small bedrooms, a bathroom, a kitchen and a living room.

I remember three distinct features about this parsonage. The first was a coal-burning stove that was the source of heat for the entire house in the winter. The small living room would be roasting hot, but my bedroom always felt like a chilly day in November. The church was also heated by a coal furnace, and did a much better job of keeping the place warm than did the small stove in our house.

The second feature I remember is the floors in the house. They were old, and the wood under the linoleum was so rotten that several women from the church who dropped in wearing pointy, high-heel shoes, found their footwear going right through the floor. Embarrassed, we would pop the shoe back out of the hole.

People soon learned that if you visited Preacher Stone's house, you would want to take your heels off before you lost a shoe or fell and broke your neck! Eventually, we raised enough money for new floors.

The third and most prominent memory I have is of the "sewer rats." We lived next to a river, and during every major rainstorm, the water would run down the mountains and empty into the river, flooding some areas. The combination of the river and the old musty wood under the house created a climate for rats.

These were not normal rats you kill in a small mousetrap. They were large beasts as long as a man's shoe. At night we could sometimes hear a clawing sound. We even heard them in the closet. They could have taped a movie from that parsonage called *The Revenge of the Rats*.

On several occasions a rat would boldly run under the couch. Dad would take his shoe and threaten to "whip it within an inch of its life." The rats would win a few, and Dad would nail some with his shoe and win a few.

Eventually, we put mousetraps throughout the house—even in the kitchen cabinets. When we would go for a box of cereal in the mornings, our small fingers had to avoid the mousetraps. We always knew when we caught one because the smell in the house would change!

Mom's parents, John and Lucy Bava, were visiting us once when Mom found several areas of rat droppings in the cabinets. (Rat "leftovers" are shaped like rice.) Granddad, always a cutup, took the opportunity to offer me my first job.

He said, "Perry I want to give you a job." At age six I was all excited about the prospect. "What is the job?" I inquired. He replied, "You can whitewash this rat dump and sell it for rice." I began jumping up and down, thinking he was serious.

I went to church and began telling my friends about the job my Granddad offered me. They just looked at me and said nothing. Of course, Dad let me know it was a joke, and that I should not be repeating this to the church members.

MANY LOW-INCOME MEMBERS

During the earlier days of the Full Gospel/Pentecostal movement, many members were common farmers, mill workers or plant workers. For some unknown reason, some Pentecostal ministers commonly taught that personal wealth was a snare; and if a person had excessive amounts of money, it was worldly and sinful. Needless to say, few business owners were drawn to the local Pentecostal churches, unless they had been raised in a Pentecostal home.

Denominational teaching usually forbade members from wearing jewelry. In earlier days, even wedding bands were taboo. The people who did attend the churches, however, were loyal, dedicated Christians whose only desire was to please God in their actions and in their appearance. The church services were always charged with prayer, praise and the presence of the Lord.

In those days Pentecostal people were often considered by society to be the "poorer class" in the community. Even some community leaders looked on Pentecostal church members as an uneducated, poorer class. When they had an emergency and needed prayer or an immediate answer from God, however, they would secretly call or come by the church and ask "Preacher Stone" to please pray for them.

Because the people were on a lower income scale, Mom and Dad were bi-vocational ministers. They both worked side jobs.

Dad also volunteered with the local rescue squad. One day he was called to a local barber shop. On arriving, Dad learned that a doctor from town had thrust his fist through a large plate glass window. Bleeding and cursing, the doctor was sitting in a chair, saying, "I am going to hell! Let me alone, I want to go to hell." As the paramedics attempted to tie a tourniquet on his arm, the raving man would tear it off.

Eventually, the police talked him into getting in the ambulance. But the paramedics refused to get in the ambulance with him, as he was still pulling on the tourniquet. Mr. Rollins, a police officer, got in the ambulance and asked Dad to ride with him. The bleeding doctor threatened to kick Dad through the ambulance window.

The officer told him, "This man is a pastor. If you hit him, I'll take this blackjack and crack your skull!" Dad told the man, "Doctor, we are here to help you. You have cut two arteries in your arm, and if you don't calm down, you will lose too much blood and die." Dad's comments helped save the man's life. The incident increased Dad's influence in the community. People would shake Dad's hand and say, "Are you the preacher who got in the ambulance with that mad man?"

One unusual incident for Dad came when a reporter, John Sherrill of *Esquire* magazine, was traveling from South Carolina looking for a story on someone who believed in healing and had been healed. John stopped at the local supermarket to buy snacks, and saw a poster announcing a revival at our church with Evangelist Glenna Jesse. She had been healed of severe heart trouble and other complications. The man called the number on the revival poster and Dad answered the phone. The reporter said:

> I have been traveling from South Carolina and have been interviewing people who believe in divine healing. Some people say they believe in it but they have never seen an actual healing. I am looking for someone who believes in it, and has seen it.

Dad said, "You have called the right people. I have an evangelist here who has been healed by the power of God." Mr. Sherrill made an appointment with Dad and Glenna at the church, and wrote a large article. He sent a photographer to take pictures, and within a few months the magazine and the article hit the newsstands.

In that issue of *Esquire* there was an article about Oliver B. Green, the well-known preacher from South Carolina. On the following pages they had the article on Fred Stone and Glenna Jesse from the mountains of Virginia. When the magazine arrived at the news counter in town, many of the well-respected business people couldn't believe that the local Pentecostal preacher at the red brick church was featured in a national magazine article. They wondered what his connections were and who he knew in such prominent places.

At school the kids asked, "Your dad is that preacher in *Esquire*? Man, your dad is famous!" I stuck out my chest, and said, "Yes, he's famous. That's my Dad." The Lord used these incidents to help Dad gain influence among the unchurched in the community. Our people were simple people, but they were praying saints who loved the Lord.

In those days there were very few men in the church, and without the women most churches would have closed the doors for lack of finances. Most women in our church did not work at outside jobs, but they did labor at the church, cooking pies and chicken dinners for fund-raisers. We may not have been known for soul winning, but we could win a blue ribbon at the country fair for those pies!

PREACHER'S KID MISCHIEF

As a minister's kid I knew people expected a higher standard from me than they did out of the deacons' children. If Diana, Phillip or I did something questionable, we would be verbally chastised by the members *and* my Dad. Because of the strict upbringing of the denomination, my sister was not allowed to wear pants, makeup or jewelry. Others attending the church might get by with it, but not the preacher's kids.

We did have friends outside the church. Some were good kids, but others were bad influences. The Boatwright boys were three brothers. Since one of them was near my age, I became friends with the two youngest. They had a major problem with cursing—they could peel the plaster off a wall with their crude and downright vulgar language. They never cursed in front of Dad, but didn't mind doing so when he was not around.

At times the Boatwright boys were bullies, and I lived in fear they would beat me up. I chose to get in with them, and their influence got me one of the worst whippings I can remember.

The church had purchased new paint to re-paint the church basement. One old wall would receive the new look first, so I asked Dad if I could take some old paint and paint on the wall before the men painted over it. He agreed and left me with a small can of paint and a paint brush.

Musing about what I would put on the wall, I thought of some of the words the Boatright boys used. I was only a first grader, and couldn't spell very well; but I gave it my best shot. When Dad returned, there, on the church wall, were vulgar and obscene words painted by the hands of his firstborn son! Before the lights went out that night, I knew that those words would be banned from my vocabulary.

I did manage to escape the sting of Dad's black belt on occasion, however. One afternoon Dad was at work, and I decided to give my teddy bear a ride in my little red wagon. I was pulling the wagon through a series of mud puddles, so I needed an extension on the wagon handle.

I looked through the house and found three of Dad's church ties he wore with his suits. I tied the ties together, and then tied one of them onto the handle of the wagon. Wow, did that ever work! Mud splattered everywhere, and the bear bounced like a rubber ball.

Soon, Dad pulled into the driveway and saw his ties. Needless to say, I was snatched up from the dirt road and marched into the house. My mind was already racing, *What could I do to avoid this whipping?*

Suddenly, I looked up at Dad, made my two front teeth protrude and made a rabbit face. I then yelled, "What's up, Doc?" He stopped and began laughing. Taking advantage of the situation, I continued my Bugs Bunny imitation, "I said, what's up Doc?" By now he was laughing hilariously, so I ran out into the yard to escape the spanking. That time it worked!

On another occasion, I got into big trouble with Dad. He went outside to bring me into the house. When I saw him coming, I spotted Mr. Moseman about 50 feet away. He was the neighbor next door.

As Dad reached for me, I slumped over like I had been shot. I yelled, "Go ahead and beat me to death. That's what you want to do anyway . . . kill me!" Embarrassed, Dad walked away. Mistakenly, I thought I had outwitted him. Late that evening I learned that Dad's memory was longer than mine. I experienced his discipline anyway.

Of course, there were a few times when I had fun with Dad and his spankings. Once, someone lied about me to get me in trouble, and Dad knew what had really happened. He took me in the house and told me, "I am going to strike the bed with the belt. You begin to holler and yell like you are being whipped!"

Did we ever give the fellow standing outside a show! He had pleasure thinking I was in trouble, when all the time Dad and I were smiling and I was yelling like I was dying. Kids today are not disciplined the way we were when we were growing up. Old-timers used a switch or a belt, and believed a good old spanking was needed every now and then. Their favorite verse was, "You shall beat him with a rod, and deliver his soul from hell" (Proverbs 23:14). If we would discipline our children today the way previous generations did, we would be reported to the social services! All four of us kids received our share of spankings growing up, and we all turned out just fine.

THE COMMUNIST FLAG

When we lived in Big Stone Gap, the Vietnam War was raging. Steve Polly was my closest church friend. Steve's dad, Jan, was in Vietnam serving as a gunnery sergeant with the Marines. Jan had seized a North Vietnamese stronghold, and sent a flag back to his son.

Steve and I enjoyed playing imaginary war games. We used sticks for guns and our lunch packs for backpacks. When the flag arrived, it was a valuable addition to our war arsenal. We hung the Communist flag on a stick, clinched our imaginary stick guns in our hands and went to war! We crossed the bridge into town and marched up and down in front of small businesses, waving the North Vietnamese flag.

We couldn't understand the strange looks we received from the townsfolk. In fact, a few became angry with us. We finally returned to the parsonage and completed the imaginary battle in the back yard. When Jan found out about our use of the flag, Steve saw stars and stripes . . . but it wasn't the American flag!

IN-HOUSE FIGHTING

Those raised with siblings know that there is always a fight to break up at home. Three of us children grew up in a small, two-bedroom house, with normal fussing occurring on a daily basis. On at least two occasions, it reached a feverish pitch. Once my sister, Diana, and I were engaged in a shouting match. It came to a halt when she shoved me toward the screen door. I hit the glass pane in the door and broke it. A six-inch piece of glass got caught in the back of my pants, but it appeared the glass had pierced my backside. I knew I wasn't hurt; I felt no pain. But I began to fake a cry, pointing to the glass pane protruding from my rear. Diana turned as pale as a ghost, and I had a brief moment of enjoyment, watching her sweat as she thought she may have hurt me.

Another event we look back on with laughter included my younger brother, Phillip. One Wednesday night, Diana and I stayed home to complete our school work. I went to the refrigerator to get some grapes. Phillip was about 4-years-old and had his own clay cereal bowl. Plopping down on the couch I refused to let Phillip have any grapes. He began crying, and suddenly flung the bowl at me so hard it hit the right corner of my head and shattered the bowl. The impact caused a half-inch gash across my head.

Diana ran to the church and got Mom. Mom grabbed me and took me to the church where Dad was preparing to preach. He saw me bleeding from my head and said, "Brother Chandler, please take over the service, there seems to be a problem." They drove me 11 miles away to Norton, where a doctor was called to put stitches in my head. Somewhere under my hairline is a light scar I still carry from the "battle of the cereal bowl."

Growing up in this small rural community brings back the fondest of memories. Our lives took a drastic change, however, when Dad received a phone call from the state overseer of the denomination.

MOVING TO THE BIG CITY

Dad received an invitation to take a church in Arlington, Virginia. He moved our family from the comfort of a rural mountain community to a major city—to us, culture shock. Most people in rural communities were family-oriented and church-attending—or respecting of people who were. We arrived in Falls Church, Virginia, to a new neighborhood, a new school and the need to make new friends. I felt insecure attending the new school.

After a year, we moved to another neighborhood in Arlington, Virginia. The early 1970's were a time of racial fighting between the blacks and the whites. My sister attended Wakefield High School, where fighting often broke out among students. I attended Kenmore Junior High.

Many of the students were, in my opinion, terrible in their attitude and respect toward authority. In some classes the teachers chose to exercise little or no control over some of their students. I was often shoved against a locker and physically threatened. On one occasion a group of boys tied my shoe laces together and made me hop around the room like a rabbit, just to humiliate me. On another occasion they spilled paint on the floor and threatened me if I didn't lick it up.

I despised public school. For me, the seventh grade was the "grade from hell." There were no Christian schools in those early days. Had one existed, I would have been the first to enroll. I consistently wanted to quit school. My grades suffered due to my lack of interest and hatred for the school and its students.

I decided if I couldn't quit school I'd get myself thrown out. One day in class I started a fire inside my metal desk. It wasn't life threatening; but when smoke began coming from the desk, the teacher yanked me up and sent me to the principal. He called my mother, who was working at a medical doctor's office, to pick me up. I was expelled for several days.

On another occasion, I was so depressed that I took a huge dose of diet pills, hoping it would send me to the hospital. Instead, I walked around in a daze for the entire day. Both seventh and eighth grades were the worst times of my young life.

STRUCK WITH MENINGITIS

By ninth grade I had made a few friends. I played football, wrestled and was on the track team. I loved sports. During the football season I became very ill. It was October, and there was no flu outbreak at the school. The headaches became severe. It felt as if my brain was on pins and needles. The doctor diagnosed it as a form of meningitis, and required me to stay in bed and take certain antibiotics. I was a starter on the team and was missing football practice.

On Thursday—game day—I took an abundance of pills and told Mom I was better. I went to school and played both tight end and defensive end throughout much of the game. After the game I walked the two miles home, went into my bedroom and collapsed. I was in serious physical condition but was afraid to tell Mom what I did. It felt as though my head would explode. When I moved, pain shot through my brain.

Thank God, we were beginning a revival and, as always, we were required to attend. I recall lying on the pew most of the service. During the altar service the evangelist called me forward for prayer, and I received an instant healing! I returned home without any pain.

For five straight years after this incident, the same symptoms of meningitis would come upon me. They would attack me in the same month, October, at almost the same week and the same day every year. It was as though a spiritual power was marking a calendar each year at the same time with the words, "Attack Perry." I struggled every year for five years—until age 18.

By the sixth year I was heavily into the Word of God. When the symptoms struck me that year, I began confessing the Word aloud and saying that I would not allow this attack to stay in my body. The Anointing literally drove the sickness from me once and for all! Since 1978, I have had no symptoms of this sickness.

THE CHURCH BUILDING BEGAN FALLING APART

The church in northern Virginia was having its own challenges. Dad assumed the pastorate of Bailey's Crossroads Church of God with about 15 active members. Through prayer and hard work, the church began to grow—to 40, then 80, and up to 150 attenders. The building was not large, but it was relatively new.

One Sunday night we heard a crashing sound coming from the vestibule. Wanda Dunford, a member of the church, came into the sanctuary with her leg partly covered in tar and gravel. The corner of the flat gravel roof in the vestibule had collapsed! Thank God, no children were standing nearby.

The roof was repaired, but weeks later we arrived at church after a rain storm and noticed that the concrete on the entire left side of the building, in all the Sunday school rooms, had collapsed about six inches. Perhaps to save money, the builder had not put wire mesh in the cement.

For a small church, the additional cost of repairs was a heavy burden. Dad attempted to get the builder to correct the mistake. Instead, the contractor convinced the local district pastor and the district overseer that Dad was causing trouble by asking the builder to correct his mistake.

Despite these hindrances God blessed the church and brought many people into the congregation. One of the most unique was a man whom I would later discover worked for the Central Intelligence Agency (C.I.A.).

The Watergate Break-In

This man, Bill Hall, was in Walter Reed hospital with cancer. His wife called Dad to see if he would come and pray for her husband. Dad went and ministered to Bill, and God touched him so that he recovered. He began attending Dad's church. What he did on his job was so secretive that his own wife did not know any details. He became very close to Dad.

On several occasions the Lord gave Bill a word through Dad that was so accurate the man knew it was from God. Bill was praying for the Baptism in the Holy Ghost, but seemed to be hindered. Dad dreamed that Bill fought and killed a foreign agent, who was a double agent. Dad could see that Bill had to defend himself or be killed. Dad told Bill the details, and learned that the entire dream was 100 percent accurate. When Bill was told that the Lord knew it was in self-defense, he received the infilling of the Holy Spirit.

One afternoon he called Dad and asked him to meet at a Hot Shop restaurant. Picking a corner booth away from people, Bill said, "Brother Stone, there was a break-in at the Watergate Apartments." Bill already knew the details, and said the *Washington Post* was going to do a news story about the break-in and it would all come back on President Nixon. Months later, as the controversial story swept across America, President Nixon was in trouble.

From time to time Bill would give Dad a few nuggets about what really went on with the Watergate break-in. According to Bill, a man in the Pentagon was making copies of the war plans for the Vietnam War and giving them to the Russians, perhaps through the Russian Embassy. When our troops planned a bombing raid, the enemy sites would have been moved to another location. They knew that someone on the inside was releasing secret information.

At the time a politician running for a high position offered the man at the Pentagon a cabinet post in his administration if he could hurt Nixon's re-election possibilities. The politician knew it would take something involving the Vietnam War to affect the voting public. The C.I.A had actually taped the conversation with the famous politician and the man at the Pentagon, and Bill had personally heard the tapes.

He said that some in the agency believed the Russians were blackmailing the man at the Pentagon, threatening to make information about him public that would, in those days, have destroyed his political future. Some believed the fellow may have told his personal psychiatrist about the blackmail scheme, and the papers would be on file in the offices at the Watergate complex.

He then told Dad something very interesting. He said, "If the American people knew all that actually went on (in this case), they would turn against a certain political party and we would have a one-party system. Nixon, however, will be the fall man because the nation cannot take the full scandal. For years to come Nixon will carry a bad name; but years from now, when all the truth comes out, people will realize Nixon was protecting the political system of America." Events unfolded just as Bill predicted. Nixon was impeached, and stepped down.

Dad never spoke much about what Bill told him until Bill passed away (the C.I.A. mandated a closed-coffin funeral for him). To this day Dad does not tell any of the stories in public. He did tell me that Bill warned him in 1974 that Islamic terrorists would be America's greatest threat in the future. He said the Agency had warned three American presidents not to allow the Muslims to pour into the country.

Many were agents of the P.L.O. and other Islamic terrorist groups, he said. But in the name of freedom, no leader was paying attention to the warnings. As long as the terrorists struck overseas, America felt safe.

Other church members worked in high government positions. Dad, Phillip and I were given tours of the Pentagon and other government facilities. We went to areas with guarded vaults, and islands where the trees had telephones in them!

Dr. Spence, a medical doctor, attended the Washington Street Methodist Church in Alexandria, the same church George Washington had attended. He began to visit our little church. During one service Dad began to pray for Dr. Spence's German fiancée, Mary Ann. As Dad began praying in other tongues through the Holy Ghost, Mary Ann gripped Dad's hands and said, "You speak perfect German!"

Dad told her he didn't know German, and the prayer was a prayer by the Holy Spirit. Mary Ann began to tell Dad word-for-word what the Spirit had prayed in the German language.

This supernatural miracle impressed the doctor, and both of them became faithful members of the church. Our family took him up on an offer to use his summer house in North Carolina for one of our family vacations.

FIVE YEARS OF SEED PLANTING

The northern Virginia years, from age 10 to 14, were the "seed-planting season" in my life. At age 11, I had received the Holy Spirit during a youth camp. I purchased a drum set through my grandfather's music company. With the help of David Nitz of the singing Nitz Family, I began teaching myself to play the drums.

I practiced playing the drums at home. This musical apprenticeship almost drove my parents and the neighbors crazy. Long before I had children I decided not one of my offspring would ever be a drummer. I wanted peace and quiet in my future house!

As my talent developed, I took the drums to the annual camp meeting to play with the camp meeting choir. I am sure the music ministers appreciated me inviting myself to be their drummer for the week! Once, two different drums were set up, and I was never told this. I'm sure the music director told the other fellow to show up, since he was more experienced than I was.

CAMP MEETING IN THE TABERNACLE

The greatest spiritual impact on me during those years was the yearly youth camps and camp meetings hosted by the denomination each summer in Roanoke, Virginia. I attended the youth camps faithfully, as both camper and counselor. The memories are numerous.

As a teenage camper, I remember lying awake at night in a dorm room with 14 other fellows, and praying while they were trying to sleep. One night a boy grabbed me and thrust me outside the door, demanding, "You can come back in when you shut up and quit praying."

After beating on the door for several minutes, I was eventually welcomed back into the group. The unsaved fellow who physically expelled me was later saved, filled with the Spirit and called into the ministry. His name is John Cahill, today a prominent pastor and teacher in South Carolina.

Campmeetings were the highlight for every preacher's kid. They were conducted in July, during the hottest part of the summer. Morning and evening services were conducted in an open-air, metal tabernacle. Every minister was required to wear a suit and tie, even if the weather was 100 degrees in the shade. Sitting in the packed tabernacle in the middle of summer made a person more appreciative of air conditioning and deodorant!

As the sun set and the darkness came to rest on the mountains, the light from the tabernacle formed a silhouette, reminding me of "a city that is set on a hill" (Matthew 5:14).

The most memorable meetings were when global evangelist T. L. Lowery was the night speaker. Dr. Lowery was an international minister with a powerful healing ministry. When it was announced he was coming, people drove for hours just to be in the service. Often the crowds swelled into the thousands, with people sitting rows deep in metal folding chairs outside the tabernacle.

When I was 11, Dr. Lowery was the night speaker at the Virginia Camp Meeting. During the altar service he formed a prayer line to minister to the sick. I spotted a man who was limping, and leaning on a cane. I ignored everyone else and glued my attention to this fellow. Would he be healed?

Eventually, the man stood face-to-face with Brother Lowery. In a flash, T. L. stripped the cane from the man's grip and slapped his anointed hand on the fellow's head. The power of God struck the gentleman to the ground, but he bounced to his feet like a rubber ball. He began running as fast as he could across the platform. Lowery threw the cane, and it went sailing in my direction, hitting the wall behind me.

At that instant, I felt the presence of the Holy Spirit for the first time in my life! My hair stood on end, and I sensed spiritual "electricity" in the atmosphere. This was the first miracle I would see, but certainly not the last.

T. L. Lowery, the Influence of a Mentor

After my call to the ministry, T. L. Lowery became a mentor to me. He has impacted my life and ministry. Years later, at age 20, I was attending the Alabama State Campmeeting, and Dr. Lowery had just concluded a 40-day fast. When the state overseer, Rev. Robert White, introduced him as the night speaker, Brother Lowery was so weak he could barely speak or stand.

After a few minutes of exhorting the people, the glory of God pierced the atmosphere in the huge metal tabernacle. People began running to the altar, and Lowery began laying hands on those all around him. Everyone he touched fell to the ground like a tree falling in a storm. That night he cast an unclean spirit out of a young woman who was growling and cursing.

The unclean spirit departed with such force that it shook the back of the tabernacle. People heard a sound like a big fist slamming into the metal building. The incident frightened those who were cold and indifferent, and brought a second wave of seekers to the altar.

Despite Dr. Lowery's dynamic anointing, some opposed his large evangelistic ministry and a few attempted to restrain his momentum by passing by-laws affecting evangelistic associations within the denomination. During a General Assembly in the 1960s, the majority of thousands of ordained ministers passed an amendment stating that no minister could have an evangelistic association within the denomination.

This affected the T. L. Lowery Evangelistic Association. Some thought Dr. Lowery would organize an independent ministry and pull hundreds of pastors out, forming his own denomination. He submitted to the regulation, however, and the same week was voted to one of the top five executive positions in the Church of God. For a time, T. L. Lowery concentrated on his new administrative responsibilities.

Years later, in the 1980's, he sought the will of God during another 40-day fast. Toward the end of the fast, an angel of the Lord appeared to him and told him to go to the Washington, D.C. area and take a small church. God said, "Whatever you build, I will fill!" Brother Lowery became the senior pastor of the National Church of God, and later built a beautiful facility in Fort Washington, Maryland. This church grew from 50 people to over 10,000 members in ten years! His ministry included an International Bible School.

I have been honored to minister at the National Church of God on many occasions, and have watched the miraculous growth of this great congregation. Growth demanded new facilities and a huge sanctuary seating up to 10,000 people is presently the home of the National Church of God.

Today, the church is pastored by Brother Lowery's son, Stephen, and continues to be a dynamic spiritual light in the Maryland-D. C. area. As a teenage minister I was often told that I would be the "next T. L. Lowery." Older people would compare our styles of ministry, the prayer lines and the anointing in the services to the early days under the Lowery tent.

I have never attempted to imitate anyone, but the dark suits, dark hair and anointed services reminded many of the early meetings under the giant tent. Mildred, Brother Lowery's wife, told me years ago, "Watching you preach is like stepping back in time many years to the days under the tent with T.L."

Dr. Lowery's magazine was the tool that inspired me to stay in touch with those who loved my ministry. His first magazine was called the *Herald of Deliverance.* I sent a newsletter out with the title *Voice of Deliverance,* but after prayer, was impressed with the name *Voice of Evangelism.*

Some ministers laughed at the name. One said, "How could a teenage preacher who had preached in only three states be the *voice* of anything, much less a voice for or of Evangelism?" Their criticism never deterred me, because the Holy Spirit sees into the future and not just the present. He saw a global ministry!

In 1978, when I began publishing a small magazine and building a mailing list, numerous pastors warned, "The denomination will not allow you to get too large. They will put the pressure on you the way they did Brother Lowery, and you'll have to take a position or pastor a church."

Despite predictions, I continued to send out a monthly newsletter and build a list of names from those who requested information on our ministry. By 2004, the four-page flyer I sent out in 1978 had evolved and grown into a bimonthly 24-page four-color magazine called *The Voice of Evangelism*. No church official ever requested that I cease publishing the magazine. I was never told to stop building a mailing list. I was always careful not to publicly ask for names from the pulpit, and only grew the list by people hearing about the publication.

Dr. Lowery had also published numerous books which inspired me to place important sermons in book form. Once again my youthful age became a stumbling block to some men who felt I was too young and inexperienced to write books.

In their opinion, an author should have journalistic experience, years of life experiences and years of spiritual maturity. Despite moments of discouragement, I continued to print several 32-page booklets with important messages.

As an 11-year-old, sitting in that hot tabernacle in July and watching T. L. Lowery minister, I would have never imagined that one day I would serve with him on the board of his international evangelistic association. The yearly camp meetings in Virginia made a lasting impression on my mind and inspired me to keep the yearly camp meetings alive by conducting our own yearly ministry campmeetings.

WE MOVE TO GREEN ACRES

After living several years in northern Virginia, Dad received a call in 1975 to a church in Salem, Virginia. I loved central Virginia, especially the beautiful mountains. Dad accepted the pastorate and we moved from the bumper-to-bumper traffic, the noise and the smog of the city to a rather peaceful, historic town located near Roanoke.

The church was well established with many wonderful, kind people. The parsonage was located next to the church and it became the brunt of jokes among us kids. We affectionately called it "Green Acres," because the wood-frame house was painted green and covered with a silver, tin roof. All of the floors throughout the house were uneven. My room had an "official" Green Acres closet, just like the television series. If you slid the door too far, it would fall off its hinges!

We only had an occasional rat. They were not nearly the size of the sewer rats in Big Stone Gap. The best thing going for the house was the musical serenade on rainy days and nights. The drops of water beating against the old tin roof created a hypnotic melody that could put you to sleep. At Salem I took on the janitorial job of the church, played the drums and helped from time to time in the bus ministry. Some of the things that seemed rather insignificant at that season of my life, I now realize, were the small seeds to major plans that God had for me.

MY FIRST SEED: GIVING UP MY DRUMS

Living in Salem, I became personal friends with missionary-evangelist Emmett Hinkley. Emmett, who lived in Roanoke, was the most gifted piano player I had ever heard. He was a prolific writer, and owned his own print shop in the basement of his house. I was fascinated with the printing presses and with how the printing system operated.

Emmett rented a building near our house, and after school I spent many hours learning the art of laying out magazines and books. I never realized that this would one day be a major part of my own ministry.

When I was about 18, I told Emmett I wanted to print a book of my own. I had a manuscript called *Precious Promises for Believers*, but had no money for the printing costs. Emmett made me a unique offer. His son, Buddy, wanted to learn to play the drums. Over several years I had purchased a substantial drum set, and was playing the drums for the choir at Dad's church. Emmett said, "Perry, I will make a deal with you. Give Buddy your drum set, and I will layout and print 500 copies of your book."

Today, this decision seems so small, but in retrospect I realize that if I had held on to the drums, I may have never planted the first seed for the outreach ministry we now have at the *Voice of Evangelism*. After prayer, I chose to give away my drums, valued at about $1,200, to print a 32-page book. I was taking what I had and creating something I didn't have. I was planting a seed for a future harvest.

The sale of this little book provided the small income which enabled me to begin writing and printing several books (now out of print). Some of them were called: *The Blessing and Curse of Anointed Music*, *The Cause and Cure for Fear and Worry*, and *Healing Though Christ*. Little did I realize that spending those days with Emmett would inspire my young vision and teach me the importance of promoting my meetings through radio, television, posters and promotional kits. He also showed me the importance of staying in touch with friends through the printed media, such as a newsletter and a magazine.

Every piece of knowledge was actually a seed planted that would one day produce fruit for the Kingdom of God through our own ministry. Relating these personal stories serves several purposes. The primary one is to make our friends and partners more familiar with the events that impacted my life and helped mold this ministry. The second purpose is to encourage those called into the ministry to pursue the purpose of God in their own lives, despite any friction or opposition they may be encountering. The third reason is to give you lesson nuggets that you can use in your own personal life.

Lessons I Have Learned in These Experiences

- ♦ God has always used those whom society considered to be common people.

- ♦ God is preparing your future, even during childhood.

- ♦ You can train yourself to do what God has called you to do.

- ♦ What you learn today may be the seed of God's will for tomorrow.

- ♦ Every person needs a mentor who can impact their life and give instructions.

- ♦ The seed you plant today is tomorrow's harvest.

- ♦ Childhood memories make great stories when you are older.

CHAPTER 4

ARE YOU REALLY CALLED, OR JUST FULL OF ZEAL?

His disciples remembered that it was written, "Zeal for Your house has eaten Me up" (John 2:17).

ARE YOU REALLY CALLED, OR JUST FULL OF ZEAL?

There are moments when you have special encounters with the Holy Spirit that birth a fresh spiritual hunger in you and thrust you to another level with God. There were three such moments in my early life.

My first encounter with the supernatural occurred at age eight. It was in my father's church in Big Stone Gap. One Sunday night, Dad began praying for a young man who was possessed with an evil spirit.

As I watched from the second pew, I could see a large, milky-looking object coming out of the young man's mouth. As it exited, the boy was instantly delivered. In retrospect, I believe I actually saw a visible form of an evil spirit departing during this act of exorcism.

The second experience was at a church youth camp in Roanoke, Virginia. I was 11 years old and full of mischief. That year, I disliked the camp so I broke the rules and sneaked away to a pay phone located at a gas station across the interstate. I phoned my mother five hours away to come and get me. She refused.

Later that night, I was caught throwing rocks on the roof of the tabernacle. The state youth director, Dick Davis, threatened to send me home, which was fine with me. Instead, he offered me "one last chance." The next night I was under great conviction, and went to the altar and prayed for over one hour. This led to my receiving the infilling of the Holy Spirit. This one event, at age 11, would be the catalyst for my entire life.

The third experience may not seem as dramatic, but it was just as important. When I was 15, my father hosted a revival in our church in Salem, Virginia. Three single men called the Victory Men Evangelistic Team came to conduct the revival. It lasted for three weeks, and helped pull the church and youth together.

Several weeks after the revival closed I dreamed I was opening a large brown-covered book. The book was a written record of the places where I had preached, including a list of the spiritual results and the offerings I had received in each location.

At the time I was not preaching, and was simply the janitor of the church! From time to time I had taught small children in Sunday school and worked in the summer vacation Bible school, but there was no call on my life, or so I thought. The revival stirred a hunger for God's presence in my life.

Sports and Architecture

At 15, my first love was sports, not God. I was consumed with football, and would avoid eating out on Sunday afternoon to watch a professional game on television. I would organize men from church to meet at the high school football field on Sunday afternoons, where we played tackle football without any protection.

Some of the men broke their arms and collar bones, and we always left the game so sore we could hardly move. I felt my future would be in the field of architecture. I enjoyed art, creating and drawing. There was good money in this profession, and Dad had a brother in Ohio, William Stone, who was a successful engineer. A good education meant a good job. This was the direction I chose for my life. Then a prayer meeting interrupted my plans.

THE ALL-NIGHT PRAYER MEETING

I was 16 years of age. One Sunday night after service, three older friends, Ted Taylor, Wayne Meade and Carlton Coffee, came to our home next door to the church for a time of fellowship. As we sipped coffee and ate a few bites of homemade cake, Dad began to share some remarkable faith-building stories of miracles he witnessed as a young minister.

As our faith began to rise, I suggested we four fellows return to the church for a brief prayer meeting. It was close to 10 o'clock at night when we knelt in the sanctuary for prayer. Time passed, and the intensity of the praying increased. The tangible presence of God began to rise. By 2 o'clock in the morning, it felt like there was an open window to heaven above the church.

We all later believed we felt the presence of an angel of the Lord among us as we entered a dimension of intercession none of us had ever experienced. Hours passed. The round clock above the double doors of the sanctuary read 3 o'clock in the morning. I stepped outside the church door, located near the right side of the altar, for a breath of fresh air. It was a clear night, and the stars sparkled millions of miles away.

At that moment I heard the still, small voice that I would hear many times on my faith journey. It said simply, "I have called you to preach." I was overwhelmed with God's presence. Moments later I stepped back into the sanctuary and announced to my three friends that God had just called me to preach. No one seemed to be excited about this new revelation. They smiled and thanked God, yet their expressions seemed to say, "Time will tell."

WAS IT JUST ZEAL, OR A TRUE CALL OF GOD?

A few days later I spoke to my father, telling him that the Lord had spoken to my heart and called me to the ministry. I was taken aback at his response. He seemed to be rather uninterested. I would bring the subject up from time to time, and he would remind me of how difficult the ministry was. Dad seemed to sow seeds of discouragement. Had my heart not been connected to the will of God and had I not known I was destined to minister the gospel, I would have resigned emotionally before I started.

Later, I discovered Dad's agenda from the outset of my announcement. He was attempting to separate the zeal of the Lord from the call of the Lord. Throughout his ministry Dad had witnessed many young men strike the hot iron and "get on fire" for the Lord.

Often the first impression of someone on fire is to preach the gospel. Some quit their jobs, only to return to another job months later. Others allow the burning embers of God's zeal to be smothered with the dust of the cares of life. Dad knew that if he could discourage me from entering the ministry, I was only experiencing a surge of zeal and not a true call from God.

Immediately, my family saw a transformation in my personal life. I began carrying my large Dake Bible to school. I would return home and spend hours listening to gospel music and studying. Mom noticed that the more I studied the Bible, the better my school grades became. After months of waiting, I gained enough courage to ask Dad if I could preach my first message at the church. He consented, and I immediately began studying and preparing a message.

On April 14, 1976, I preached on the subject, "After the Holy Ghost, What Then?" By the conclusion of the service, I knew I was called to preach. It was not because the message was a great message or because there were altar results, but because I felt a true, inner peace.

A few months passed and the fellows from the prayer meeting inquired, "When are you going to quit *talking* about being called to preach and *start preaching*?" In those days, as today, few pastors would open their pulpits to young ministers who had just started in the ministry.

Pastors are protective of their flocks, and they should be. An inexperienced minister can beat the sheep instead of feed the sheep. It may take a local pastor weeks of explanation to undo the seed planted in a single service by an immature minister.

I had one contact, Grandfather John Bava, who pastored a small, rural church in Gorman, Maryland. The church was organized by my father and granddad in June 1959, the same week in which I was born. I called Granddad and asked him if I could come up to the church. He thought I wanted to bring my set of drums and play. I said, "No I want to preach."

I had one blue suit jacket and I was scheduled for three services. I borrowed Mom's blue Ford, not knowing that the seal around the gas tank was causing fuel to leak out. I filled the car up, and immediately gas began dripping out beneath the vehicle. I had no choice but to go on; and I lost half the fuel on the five-hour drive to Davis, West Virginia, where Granddad lived.

This was the first time I traveled to preach. About 15 people showed up to hear "little Perry" preach on that warm, summer night. I remember reading the opening scripture and not being able to pronounce the word *sumptuously* in Luke 16:19. After stumbling for a few seconds, I picked up on my thoughts and continued. I did more exhorting than preaching.

A year later, my grandfather said that after the service, he didn't sleep all night. He called my dad and said, "Fred, you need to get this boy licensed in the ministry. He has a gift to preach!"

During the summer months I worked at the church campground for a little over $2 an hour. I mowed grass and assisted the groundskeeper with maintenance. The property was so large that once we finished mowing, it was time to start over again. My pay was poor but I enjoyed the outdoors.

One day I hiked a rugged trail behind the campground to the back of the mountain, overlooking a huge man-made lake. Pulling 12 stones from the ground, I built a personal altar next to a high, buzzing power line. Later, I bought a small brush and some paint and painted three names of God—*Jehovah Shammah, Jehovah Ro'i* and *Jehovah Ropheka.*

I painted the date to mark the dedication of my secret prayer altar: April 2, 1978. I snapped a picture to capture this special meeting place. Years later I was thumbing through old photographs and came across the black-and-white picture of the altar. I was amazed when I realized that four years after erecting this altar, on April 2, 1982, I was married to my wonderful wife!

My First Major Decision

My first major decision would come in my senior year of high school. This decision would pave the path I would follow to the full-time evangelistic ministry. During my final two years of high school, I traveled on weekends and preached by invitation. The principal of Andrew Lewis High School permitted me to check myself out early on Fridays and check in late on Mondays, due to my traveling.

Local services, prayer meetings and youth services were all parts of my "itinerary." Despite my youth and inexperience, it seemed that in every meeting the Lord would bless and His anointing would manifest itself in the services.

After completing high school, I had a crucial decision to make. In our denomination a young minister is expected to attend the denominational college. I spent two days scoping out the college, and returned home to pray and fast about what I should do. I could attend the school, or participate in external studies that would take many years to complete a B.A. degree. During a time of prayer, the Holy Spirit spoke something that seemed strange at the time. I did not talk about it for years, because I received repercussions when it inadvertently leaked out once. My decision was sealed when the Holy Spirit clearly spoke to me:

> I want you to go into full-time ministry. Spend much time in prayer and study. In the future, I am going to do things through your ministry—so great, that if you were to attend the college, some will take credit for your ministry and claim they helped to "make your ministry." If you will follow My plans, in the future men will say, "The Lord raised him up," and I will receive all the glory for your life and ministry.

This was a strange word for someone who had only preached about 20 times! I mentioned it to a few ministers, and one pastor said to me in a hateful tone, "If you don't go the way of the system, you will never amount to anything." He walked out the door of the Virginia State Office in Roanoke, and I have never seen him since.

Going God's way was difficult. Pastors continued to put pressure on me to follow the way of the church system. Instead, I chose to enter full-time ministry at age 18, and take extended college studies while traveling. The decision proved—100 percent— to be God's will.

Soon, the revivals in West Virginia and southwestern Virginia went from a few nights to many weeks in length. The attendance would begin small, but soon, crowds of people would fill the churches. Word spread that the "Stone boy" was having great revivals, and many souls were being converted and filled with the Spirit. It took more than zeal to sustain me. It took confidence that I was called of God. Despite the spiritual results, these were some of the most difficult times of my life—for several reasons.

First was the fact that I am more of an introvert than an extrovert. There I was, driving long distances to fill revival appointments to preach to people I had never met. I was staying in homes I had never been in, with people I didn't know. When I would arrive, a great spirit of heaviness would overwhelm me.

I would spend from morning until church time in the bedroom with a pile of books, my Bible and my notebooks. I prayed and studied, literally, all day. Sometimes I would skip dinner, not because I was fasting, but because I was too depressed or too shy to talk with people.

I never doubted God's call on my life, but at times I would ask myself, "How can God use me?" The insecurity I had when I considered my inner weakness was beyond belief. The struggle became more intense as time progressed. In fact, the greatest supernatural battle of my life struck about the time I was experiencing extended meetings. It was the enemy's first major attempt to silence me through intimidation.

An Unexpected Demonic Attack

It was July 15, 1978. I was 19 years old and was preaching in Weyanoke, West Virginia. As usual, I was spending substantial time in prayer and fasting. One night after retiring for the evening, the four walls in the bedroom seemed to move in on me. I began praying, and eventually went to sleep. A few weeks later I traveled to my grandparent's home in Davis, West Virginia, to minister in the area.

One night, while lying in bed, it felt as though a small pile of bedbugs had joined me. I flipped on the light and threw back the covers to discover clean white sheets. This happened again the next night, so I finally decided to sleep downstairs to avoid whatever this "agitation" was.

After this incident, I returned home to Salem for three days, tired and unconcerned about the strange events. I recall going to my bedroom in the basement one night, turning off the lights and lying down. Immediately, a cold, evil presence was in the room. It was so real I began to audibly rebuke it in Jesus' name.

After a few minutes, the presence departed and so did my sleep . . .at least for a short time. As I turned off the light the next night, the presence entered the room again. This time it seemed stronger. Again, I began praying, and rebuked it in Christ's name. It lingered longer, but in minutes the dark presence lifted from the room.

On the third night this strange presence manifested itself again. I finally decided to sleep upstairs in my younger brother, Phillip's, room. The next morning he awoke and said, "What are you doing sleeping here?" I didn't feel like explaining so I just shrugged my shoulders.

My schedule continued to be full, and I would travel to another revival and return home for a few days. Each time I returned home this same presence would manifest itself at night. It didn't seem to be present during the daytime, but would reveal itself late at night. I was fasting consistently and praying long hours. I began to wonder if perhaps I was tapping into the spirit world, or if I was under a direct attack from some form of spiritual power which I had never encountered.

A TORMENTING SPIRIT

Weeks later, I was lying on the couch reading my Bible, when I fell asleep. I awakened to a strange buzzing noise ringing in my ears. I opened my eyes, and was unable to move.

Suddenly, I heard a deep male voice audibly cursing me. It said, "We are going to get that preacher . . . we are going to get him." I opened my mouth to scream for my father and nothing came out. I lay there, pretending I'd heard nothing—as if the voice would cease if I ignored it. Fear instantly gripped my mind and spirit.

This type of manifestation began to happen once a week. Then it progressed to twice a week, and eventually, three or four times a week. When I would hear the noise and the voices, my body would "freeze" for about 10 seconds. The attacks began when I was at home, but eventually began to occur when I was traveling and staying in other people's homes.

I began to realize that this was some type of "tormenting spirit." I found myself wanting to stay up all night to avoid hearing the voices. I would sleep later in the mornings in order to stay up late at night. My physical body finally weakened, and my mind and spirit were on edge.

In November 1978, I was conducting a revival at the North Danville Church of God. Asleep in the upstairs guest room of the parsonage one night, I was awakened at 3 o'clock in the morning. I noticed that on my left side, the curtains were blowing and the window was open.

I thought, *I must have left the window open before going to sleep.* I realized, however, that it was November, and about 10 degrees outside, and I would never have opened the window!

As I sat up in the bed, I saw two dark beings come though the window and begin forming at the foot of my bed. I heard the audible voice of one say to the other, "Don't tell that preacher man we are here." I began trembling in the bed, and began to question why all this was happening.

The attacks and manifestations became so common that I began to be deceived into thinking this would be my lot in life, my "thorn in the flesh." I began to accept the fact that these spirits were assigned to me to torment me and to keep me praying and fasting.

I began to resign myself to the fact that my entire life would be spent dealing with these dark forces, these unwelcome intruders of spiritual evil. I saw no other reason for the attacks and knew no remedy to stop them.

UNDERSTANDING THE CONFLICT

Five months into this demonic assault, I was ministering in Blacksburg, Virginia. Pastor Jim Angel was a noted tent revivalist and was familiar with the ministry of Bible deliverance and with the spirit world. I felt Jim may have some understanding as to what this was about. During the revival, I chose to tell Jim the details of my experience and asked if he could discern the reason for such an uncommon spiritual conflict.

As I explained the situation, Jim said, "Perry I believe I have a word for you." He continued, "I believe it is similar to Job. The Lord has been bragging on you as He did Job. Satan has been permitted to attack you in an attempt to show God that you will back down and not be faithful to your call. This attack is to cause you to back up from what you believe and preach."

Jim's words were quickened to my spirit. I drove back to Salem with a fresh determination that I would remain faithful to God and to my ministry calling, despite every fiery dart of the wicked one. I would stand—"having done all, to stand" (Ephesians 6:13). However, as fall turned into winter, it seemed the battle only intensified.

THE REVELATION THAT BROUGHT DELIVERANCE

For six months—from July to December—I continued to endure this mental barrage without any knowledge of how to stop it. I rebuked it, I prayed about it and I quoted scripture, but I couldn't get the voices, the apparitions and the fear to cease.

Finally, the end of the year arrived. During Christmas that year, my grandparents came to Salem for a visit. The house was filled with loving family members and relatives. The sleeping arrangements changed, and my brother was assigned to sleep downstairs in my room. There were two bunk beds, one near the window and the other near the opposite wall. I chose the window and Phillip was stuck with the bed near the wall.

On December 31, 1978, moments before midnight, I knelt beside my bed and prayed the most sincere and fervent request I had ever prayed to God.

> Heavenly Father, I do not know or understand why I have been experiencing these attacks from these evil spirits for the past six months. We are coming into a New Year, and I am asking you for a new beginning. In the name of Jesus Christ, please stop these attacks and give me victory from this moment on!

I slid under the sheets and went to sleep, looking for my first good night's rest in many months. Hours later I was awakened by a hand pulling on my right leg, attempting to drag me out of bed! I tilted my head toward the dresser to check the time. The digital clock said it was 3 o'clock in the morning. At first I thought my brother was playing a trick on me. However, as I turned to his bed, I could see his silhouette by the nightlight, indicating he was sound asleep.

At that instant, I saw the face of a person appear about three feet from my head. It was as though you held a large, life-size black-and-white negative up to a light. The face began to form and I observed a masculine, peaceful image of a man. I thought, *This may be an angel! Perhaps the Lord has sent a messenger to help me.* As the thought went through my mind, the face suddenly became contorted and evil. I heard a wicked laughter that filled the air in a mocking fashion. The eyes of this being took on a deep shade of red, which I sensed was a visible manifestation of the hate it represented.

At that moment something happened to turn the battle. I felt the Holy Spirit rise up within me. I also felt my own spirit rise up at the same time. From within me I could hear the words, "No! No more of this! We will not accept this any more!" Verbally, nothing came out of my mouth, but it flowed out of my inner spirit.

Instantly, the laughing ceased and the image vanished into thin air. An anointing vibrated through my entire body. I felt the battle turn. It was as though the enemy was on the run. At that moment, I heard the Holy Spirit say these words to me:

Son, as long as you live Satan will use what you see, what you hear and what you feel against you. It is time for you to stand on the one thing that will never alter and never change: Stand on My Word!

The word was clear and to the point. I was allowing my emotions to control my feelings. If the attendance in a church was good, I felt they wanted a revival; but if people did not come out, I was discouraged. I lived in depression and fear. God knew that I, with my insecurity, could never accomplish the fullness of His purpose.

The Lord allowed these attacks to teach me that emotions and feelings would not stop them, but the power of God's Word would. That night my inner spirit came into agreement with the Holy Spirit and raised up a standard against the enemy (Isaiah 59:19).

QUIT TALKING ABOUT DEMONS

At this time my mother was working in Roanoke at the Church of God State offices. She was a State Secretary for the Reverend Floyd Lawhon, state evangelism director. Years later, Brother Lawhon told me that my mother went to him privately, seeking his advice. She said, "Brother Lawhon, I need some help with my son, Perry. He has been called into the ministry and is having great revivals. However, he is spending a lot of time studying and preaching about demons and evil spirits. Can you help him?"

Floyd met with me and began to give me this advice. "Perry, if all you do is talk about demons, then demons will show up. If you preach and talk about Jesus, than Jesus will show up." He suggested that I spend more time studying the words of Jesus than being overly concerned about the power of demons.

With his advice and the special word from the Holy Spirit, I began studying the Bible at least four, sometimes up to 14, hours every day. I poured over the notes in my Dake Bible and always carried numerous religious books with me to every meeting. I focused on filling my mind and spirit with the knowledge of the Lord. The demonic manifestations ceased; and when they have attempted to return, the Word of God rises up within my spirit to immediately lift a standard against the enemy.

The second bit of advice Brother Lawhon gave me concerned my prayer life. At 18, I returned from a four-night revival in Charlottesville, where one person had received Christ. When I told Brother Lawhon about the single soul, he said, "If you want more results from God, you must spend more time with God than you do fellowshiping with people." His words stung. Consequently, I began spending one to three hours a day in prayer, which increased the Spirit's anointing. I began seeing 50 and more converted in every meeting, and as many as 500 filled with the Holy Spirit! The Lord used Brother Lawhon to speak faith into my life.

He took me under his wing and began recommending me for revivals in local churches. His influence with pastors went far in opening doors during the early years of my ministry. Other attacks came in different forms, but God was there to warn and instruct me. After a quarter of a century of ministry, I can say that the all-night prayer meeting may have begun with zeal, but it concluded with a call into the ministry.

Lessons I Have Learned in These Experiences

- Be willing to change *your* plans when God gives you *His* plans.
- The call of God will sustain you when zeal runs out.
- The enemy will always take notice when you are entering your destiny.
- Attacks will change as your ministry walk with God does.
- Spend more time with God than with people before you minister.

CHAPTER 5

ENCOUNTERS WITH THE PROPHET OF GOD

Elisha said, "Please let a double portion of your spirit be upon me" (2 Kings 2:9).

ENCOUNTERS WITH THE PROPHET OF GOD

L et me tell you about a man who could have become the most noted Pentecostal minister of my father's generation, had he been promoted on a national level and given the opportunity of traveling the nation. Instead, he limited his travels to the coal fields of Southern West Virginia, ministering in rural churches and to individuals who sought out his prayers.

The man's name was Rufus Dunford. Uncle Rufus, as he was affectionately called, was Nalva Stone's brother. His ministry was birthed during an amazing miracle that occurred in his life.

In 1932, he was diagnosed with a brain tumor, and sent to Johns Hopkins Hospital in Baltimore. After further examination he was told that if the surgery succeeded, he could be confined to a wheelchair for life. If the surgery failed, he could be a vegetable for life. He refused the operation, resigning himself to his fate, and returned to West Virginia.

THE WHIRLWIND AND THE HEALING

The Pentecostal Movement was sweeping through the rural community where Rufus lived, and had gripped the heart of his wife, Mamie. She suggested to her ailing husband that he spend time praying and asking God for help. He fasted for three days, praying that if there was a God, He would have mercy because he didn't want to leave his wife and children.

Rufus went to the potato patch to dig a few potatoes for dinner, and as he reached for a potato, something remarkable happened. He told me:

> Suddenly I felt a wind, like a whirlwind engulf me. The power was so overwhelming that it knocked me off my feet. As I lay on my back I started praying, and the more I prayed, the better I felt.

> Suddenly I received the gift of the Holy Ghost, and began to speak in other languages through the Holy Spirit. The Spirit of the Lord began to quote the entire 16th chapter of Mark, word-for-word, as it is written in the English Bible.

The women preparing dinner peered through the kitchen window and saw Rufus lying on his back in the field. Thinking the tumor had ruptured, they ran outside and heard him praying and quoting the Bible. This was remarkable because he only had a third-grade education and could not read! They realized the brain tumor had not ruptured, but that Rufus had received a divine visitation from heaven.

He left the potato patch, saved, healed and filled with the Spirit. God had promised him the gift of tongues as a "sign to the unbeliever." After this experience, Rufus could go to any foreigner and speak to him fluently in his native tongue—*as the Holy Spirit directed him.*

At that time many immigrants from various European nations worked in the coal mines. Many spoke little or broken English, and God raised up Rufus to proclaim the gospel message to those who otherwise would have never heard it.

Because he spoke fluent Greek and Latin through the gift of the Holy Spirit, some foreign miners from Europe thought he was a Catholic priest, and called him "Father Dunford." His own children recall seeing him going up to people on the street and speaking to them in their own language. They thought it was normal for their dad to do this. Instead, it was a supernatural sign to the unbeliever that God was real!

MIRACLES IN THE MEETINGS

Fred Stone, my father, was honored to spend quality time praying with and ministering alongside this honorable man of God. In the 1950s, both men were in Beefhide, Kentucky. Dad saw Rufus pray for a 10-year-old boy who had been born with a deformed foot.

Nothing happened on the first night. Rufus called for a day of fasting and prayer. Dad said he and Rufus spent much of the following day seeking God. That night, as Rufus prayed and rubbed the boy's ankle, the bones in the foot began to pop and the ankle straightened up! The little fellow began weeping uncontrollably, and ran for the first time in his life!

Rufus also had great success praying for people with warts. After prayer, the warts would literally fall off on the floor, usually within 30 minutes. On several occasions Dad saw Rufus speak to foreigners in their own language. He would actually carry on a conversation, witnessing to them about Christ in their native tongues. As a child and as a young man, I remember meeting with Rufus at his home in West Virginia. I remember Dad telling about remarkable miracles he saw in Rufus' ministry.

In the 1970s, Rufus was admitted to Grace Hospital in Welch, West Virginia. As he lapsed in and out of consciousness, he would be praying in other tongues through the Holy Spirit. On one occasion his wife entered the room and saw four doctors standing around the bed. Her concerns were eased when she heard one of the doctors talking about Rufus praying in Greek and Latin.

"Mrs Dunford, your husband must be a very educated man," commented the doctor. "Why do you think that?" Mamie asked. The doctor said, "We have been observing him for some time. He comes in and out, and each time he is praying in Greek and Latin. It takes several years to learn this language. He is quoting scriptures from the Bible and talking about the Messiah. Was he a professor at a religious university?"

Mamie laughed out loud and said, "He never went to school much. He has a third-grade education. He was healed of a brain tumor in the 1930s and received the Holy Ghost. God gave him the gift of speaking these languages."

The doctors looked at one another and began excusing themselves from the room. It seemed they didn't want to hear about an uneducated man who had a supernatural gift from God. Rufus was sent home from the hospital, and spent his last months in a hospital bed in the living room of his house.

My Encounter with the Prophet

At age 20, I had concluded a 23-night revival in Pulaski, Virginia, and had not seen Rufus for about seven years. I felt an urgency that I must travel across the mountains and meet with him. I specifically wanted him to pray for me. I invited my friend, Paul, and my brother, Phillip, to go with me. We traveled for several hours up the winding roads to War, West Virginia, arriving in early afternoon.

After searching for a time, we discovered that Rufus's home had burned to the ground. We didn't know where he had moved. I thought, *Have I missed God? Was this just my own desire?* Instead of turning around and going back home, I enquired at the corner restaurant.

This was a small, rural town, and I was certain someone would know the whereabouts of Rufus Dunford. Inside, a waiter was wiping down the counter with a wet rag. I interrupted him and asked, "Do you know where Rufus and Mamie Dunford live? Their house burned down, and I need to find them."

"Sure" the man replied, continuing to rub the counter. "He lives in the white house on the hill. Cross the railroad tracks and you'll find him there." He pointed to a row of houses lining the hillside.

My excitement began to build, as we drove about 50 yards and parked the car just below the railroad tracks. As we walked up the path to the front door, I was anxious because we were coming unannounced. I knew that most folks in the mountain readily receive company without complaining, however.

I didn't want to intrude on someone's personal plans, so I knocked on the door and waited with bated breath for a response. The screen door opened and Mamie, Rufus's wife, stared at us for a moment and suddenly announced, "Oh my, look who is here!"

Smiling, she stepped aside to welcome us into their white frame house. As I stepped inside, I saw an old man lying in a hospital bed in the corner of the room. I recognized Rufus. Suddenly, he raised both of his skinny arms into the air and said, "I perceive the presence of a man of God in this room." His comment stunned me; I felt like weeping. Rufus didn't look toward the door so he didn't know who had entered the house, but his inner spirit was quickened by our presence.

"Who is it?" he asked his wife.

"It is Freddy Stone's boy," she said, with excitement in her voice. "You remember Freddy don't you?"

"Of course I do," he affirmed. I walked over to his bedside.

"Rufus, how are you doing?" I asked. His eyes were set back in his head in a manner that made you think he could see right into your soul. I took him by the hand.

"Oh my," he grinned. "So you're Freddy's boy? I haven't seen you in a long time."

We began to reminisce about the early days of his ministry. He asked his wife to bring a picture album showing black-and-white photos of various people who had been healed through the years of his ministry. As we turned the pages, every picture had a testimony of healing linked to the person in the picture. His wife remembered the cancer on her leg.

After prayer, the cancer was gone by the next day, and new "baby skin" had grown over the hole where it had been. As she told the story, she would would point to the spot on her leg where many years ago a cancer was healed by the prayer of faith.

His wife's testimony led him to discuss cancer, and how to pray for someone with the disease. His theology on healing was that most sickness was caused by some type of spirit, such as a spirit of sickness or infirmity. He said there was a "spirit of cancer." He explained:

> Cancer cells have a spirit attached to them. A person must rebuke the spirit of cancer and then command the cancer cells to die and the good cells to live.

His explanation was simple, yet it produced results. His theology on healing had divided some Pentecostals in the coal fields, but the many miracles of his ministry proved his prayers worked, despite theological disagreements. Minutes turned into hours, and I felt it was time to go. "Rufus, I want you to pray for me before I leave," I requested, humbly.

Before I could get another word out of my mouth, the old prophet of God began to speak in other tongues, the prayer language of the Holy Spirit. As the Holy Spirit came on him, it seemed he was turned into another man. I leaned closer to him so he could place both hands on my head.

The more he prayed in the Spirit, the stronger his voice became. I could sense an overwhelming presence of God in, on and around me. Suddenly, he stopped in the middle of the prayer. His piercing eyes were glued to mine, and he demanded to know, "What was the Holy Spirit saying?"

Honestly, I had no clue. During my 18 years, I had heard hundreds of thousands of people pray in other tongues but not once had I personally asked the Lord for an interpretation. I replied hesitantly, "I am not sure what the Spirit was saying." This was not the answer he was looking for!

He immediately rebuked me, and said, "You need to know the language the Spirit is praying in, and learn how to interpret what the Spirit is saying." He then said, "The Holy Spirit was speaking in the Latin language." I knew he was not guessing. My father had seen him do this many times, and Rufus always knew the language he was praying and the nationality of the person he was witnessing to when the Spirit of the Lord came on him.

After this divine interruption, Rufus began another prayer in the prayer language of the Holy Spirit. The prayer was fervent. As he continued to touch my head, I began feeling a warm sensation engulfing my entire body. It was the same feeling you get when your arm or leg goes to sleep because of lack of circulation. The feeling, like warm liquid fire, deep in my bones, was powerful.

My immediate thought was that I was receiving an impartation, or a transfer, of Rufus's anointing. I knew now that this was why I had traveled to West Virginia. I had not told Rufus why I came, but while I was meditating on this thought the Holy Spirit broke through again. Rufus stopped and spoke in English: "What was the Holy Spirit saying?" I was not about to be ignorant twice, so I immediately said, "He is praying that I will receive your anointing and be used in the gifts."

Without blinking an eye he blurted out, "That's it. That's right." At that moment the Spirit of the Lord came on both of us, and we began rejoicing and worshiping the Lord together. My face and hands were still tingling as though the anointing of the Spirit was moving into the very bones of my body.

My last memory of the man of God was looking back at him lying in the corner of his living room, on a hospital bed. He was staring at the door and still mumbling under his breath, saying quiet words in the language of the Holy Spirit. As we walked out of the house, one of the young men with me was still absorbing the atmosphere he had encountered. The car engine leaped to life for the journey home, but I knew my spiritual journey was only beginning.

As we drove toward Virginia, the story of Elijah and Elisha entered my mind. Elisha asked the prophet, Elijah, for a double portion of his anointing (2 Kings 2). The anointing was not tangibly manifest until Elijah was taken to heaven. For some reason, I felt the special anointing and spiritual gifts in the life of Rufus would manifest in my ministry only after his death. I knew something tangible had been imparted into my spirit, just as Paul transferred spiritual gifts to Timothy, through the laying on of hands (2 Timothy 1:6).

THE ANOINTING WAS TRANSFERRED

Three months after the encounter with Rufus, in early July, the Virginia Church of God Camp meeting was in full swing. Evangelists usually filled their traveling itineraries during this yearly church convention. At the conclusion of the meeting, standing on the stage with my black suit drenched in perspiration, I was fervently seeking God for His direction.

My father made his way toward me, carefully leaned over and said, "The Holy Spirit just told me that you are about to see miracles occur in your ministry." We hugged and wept together. Returning home late that evening, we received a phone call that Rufus Dunford had passed away that very day—at about the same time Dad whispered in my ear the word about miracles coming to my ministry!

It was now time to see if the anointing of Rufus had been transferred, or if he had carried it to the grave with him. The proof of any prophetic word is whether it comes to pass. Dad said miracles were about to happen.

A few weeks after camp meeting, I was conducting a revival in Seven Mile Ford, Virginia. During this revival a young man attended who was related to the wife of the pastor of the church. The boy had been in Johns Hopkins Hospital (the same hospital Rufus visited in 1932-33 for the brain examination). This boy was a skinny teenager whose grandfather had physically carried him into the revival service that night. His feet were wrapped in gauze, and he was unable to walk or stand without the aid of crutches.

That night I felt impressed to go to his seat and pray for him. Immediately, the fellow stood to his feet and walked, by himself, down the aisle of the church! The pastor's wife had helped wrap his feet prior to the service. The gauze was loose and she unwrapped it to examine his feet. She kept saying, "This is remarkable. This is amazing. Look at his feet!"

The next day, the young man and I went outside the church parsonage and played some basketball. This miracle was a visible confirmation that the prophetic word was true, and that the prayer of Rufus was now being answered by the Lord.

INCREASE IN PRAYING IN THE SPIRIT

The apostle Paul said, "I thank my God I speak with tongues more than you all" (1 Corinthians 14:18). He also said, "I will pray with the spirit, and I will also pray with the understanding" (v. 15). My father said Rufus would pray at least an hour a day, sometimes up to three hours three times a day. He often prayed privately in the prayer language of the Sprit, praying in an unknown tongue. Dad said when Rufus began praying in the Holy Spirit, he would pray in this prayer language until he felt the anointing lift.

I remember Dad throughout my life, spending quality time in prayer. He often prayed in the house, and he took the liberty to pray quite loud. He never quenched the Holy Spirit for fear of what the neighbors would think. When Dad and I stay in hotels, he will get "lost in the Spirit" while praying. He has no concept of time, and is little concerned what those in the rooms next to him may think.

I received the gift of the Holy Spirit at age 11 in a youth camp, but from age 11 to 15, I did not pray much in the prayer language. As my travel schedule increased, I noticed I was praying less in English and more in the Holy Spirit. As I would pray, my mind would be illuminated to fresh revelation from Scripture. I saw a steady anointing flowing in the preaching during the nightly services. The spiritual results were increasing in the altar services. From the late 1970s into the early 1980s, the revivals were extending from one to three, four and five weeks in length.

Dad and I knew that the prominent gift that he and Rufus had flowed in was the gift of "different kinds of tongues" and interpretation of tongues (1 Corinthians 12:7-10). On several occasions Dad prayed for individuals from a foreign nation in their own language. This same gift began to operate in my revival services. One of the great miracles of my early ministry involved the gift of different kinds of tongues.

The Syrian Professor and the Gift of Tongues

October 31, 1981 was Halloween and it was Saturday night, so I assumed the attendance would be weak. Instead, the Bob White Boulevard Church of God in Pulaski, Virginia, was buzzing with excitement that night. More than 600 people came to experience the blessings of the Lord.

After the choir and the offering, I went to the pulpit and began to sing an old song, "Beulah Land." As the intensity of the anointing increased, I began praying in the most unusual prayer language of the Holy Spirit I had ever heard. I remember putting down the microphone, and heading down the right aisle to pray for individuals who had formed a prayer line. When the service concluded, one of the youth leaders, Shelby Mitchell, approached me. She said, "Perry, earlier when you were speaking with tongues, it sounded like you said the words *mercy* and *grace* in the French language, but you weren't speaking French."

"Do you know the French language?" I inquired.

"I take French in college. Did you know what the Spirit of God was saying when you were praying?" she asked.

Hesitantly, I said, "I was preparing to pray for people, and I am sure He was praying for the people I was about to minister to."

She then had a strange request: "Perry, I would like to take this tape to my French teacher at Radford University. He speaks several languages. I would like for him to listen, to see if he knows exactly what was being said." Personally, I didn't like the idea of an unbeliever dissecting the words of the Holy Spirit, but I consented: "Sure. Let me know what he tells you."

A few days later, my prayer time in the sanctuary was interrupted by the church secretary, Susan Hall: "Perry, can you talk to Shelby? She is on the phone." I immediately thought of the cassette tape she took to her professor. I picked up the phone in the office and greeted Shelby.

"Perry, I need to come to the church to see you. Wait until you hear this, you are not going to believe it," She said in a nervous, yet excited, voice.

"What has happened? Is this about the tape?" I inquired.

"Yes. I took it to my professor and he gave it to another fellow who translated it!"

"Translated it?" Now she had my curiosity and my attention.

"If you are going to be at the church, I am coming right over!"

Hanging up the phone, I called a few of the church staff together, and we waited in the secretary's office. Moments later Shelby entered the office in a speed somewhere between a fast walk and a trot. She began to talk:

I just returned from having lunch with a professor who speaks fluent French and a man born and raised in

Syria, but who is in America studying Indian artifacts over in Blacksburg. His name is Mikkel Mirtaheri. I took the tape to my professor, and he said the language you spoke was a Middle Eastern dialect. He could not translate it, so he gave it to Mikkel who is originally from Syria.

By now we were captivated, and anxious to hear the rest of the story. "Go ahead," I said, "tell me the rest."

Well, Mikkel listened to the tape. I did not put all of the church service on it, just the section where you were speaking in tongues. Mikkel asked me what I was doing listening to a rabbi give a lecture when I did not understand what he was saying!

"So he understood the language?" I asked. Shelby held up a piece of paper, handwritten in blue ink:

Yes. He had this piece of paper. He said that the language on the tape was Aramaic. There are two forms of Aramaic: Chaldean and Syriac Aramaic. He was amazed that anyone would understand the form of Aramaic used by the rabbi on the tape, since he said the speaker was speaking in the old form. He believes this was the same form spoken in the time of Abraham!

I interrupted, "If it is such an older form, how did he understand it?"

Because some of his relatives in Syria still speak it to this day!

On the paper, Mikkel had penned information about the Syriac and the Chaldean forms of the Aramaic language. One was an eastern dialect and the other was a western dialect. He also noted that historically, portions of the Biblical Books of Ezra and Nehemiah had been written in the Aramaic language. What followed was the dramatic highlight. Shelby laid the paper down to show us this translation.

> The messenger of the Lord has interrupted to deliver to a people the message of the Highest Father. His love is everlasting. His mercy is longsuffering and enduring. His grace flows freely. Healing was blood-bought by His son. Deliverance power is sent forth by Jesus Christ to all people who will hear it this day.

We were stunned! "What did you do when he showed you this?" I questioned.

> I told them both that it was not a rabbi giving a lecture, but a 22-year-old preacher, born in West Virginia, who butchers the English language when he preaches. Of course they both asked how this was possible, and I attempted to explain about the Holy Spirit and how He gives us languages we can pray in.

We all began to rejoice! Usually, when a person speaks in tongues from the pulpit, it is to be interpreted unless an unbeliever can understand the language that is being spoken. Then it is a "sign to the unbeliever" (1 Corinthians 14:22). This incident proved the point. There was no need for an interpretation during the service because this event seized the attention of the unbeliever.

In January, 1982, two and a half months later, Shelby called me in Alabama to tell me that Mikkel had a supernatural encounter with the Lord at a convention in Washington State. On the phone he said, "Little lady, I found old-time religion." It was evident that God had set up this miracle to touch the heart of this man.

MARKING A TERRORIST ATTACK

The Holy Spirit can also show you things to come (John 16:13). One of my most dramatic memories of the gift of tongues is of the time the Holy Spirit marked the site of a future terrorist attack in Israel. Since 1985 we have hosted tours to Israel. We journey each year to the Holy Land during the week of Thanksgiving. Since our initial tour in 1985, we have carried thousands of Americans to the Land of God to experience the sights, sounds, smells and excitement of the land of the Bible. Often, Americans are apprehensive to make the pilgrimage, due to news reports coming from the area.

Years ago I petitioned the Lord in prayer to give me a clear word concerning my trips to Israel. He gave me the same statement he gave to Joshua when he was leading the Hebrews into the land of milk and honey. There were walled cities and giants. However, God told Joshua:

> Do not be afraid, nor be dismayed, for the Lord your God is with you wherever you go (Joshua 1:9).

This scripture became a *Rhema* word that was etched into my spirit. We have directed Holy Land groups during some of the toughest times in recent years, including six weeks before the Gulf War in 1991. One reason we continue to travel is because we trust the Holy Spirit to direct our movement.

On one occasion we were scheduled to eat lunch the following day in Haifa. That evening I went to tour director Robert Vandermaten and told him I felt we should not go to Haifa. Lunch was preplanned, but I was determined to skip the city in exchange for another area. He cancelled the lunch and planned a lunch near the Dead Sea.

The following day, at lunch time, a huge hail storm struck the city of Haifa. Hailstones were as large as softballs, and knocked out the windshields of many buses! We would have been in Haifa at the time the storm hit, but the Lord knew this and protected the group.

During another tour, we led the group into the heart of the Judean Wilderness to an old Greek monastery. A Jewish believer, Israel Aerobauch, and his Greek wife, Efroseni, were with us that morning. I sent the tour group up the hill to the monastery, and had Efroseni lead them inside where she would interpret for the monks. Israel and I sat on a sidewalk between the rugged, barren, brown mountains and the monastery, observing the beauty.

We both sensed an anointing to pray. We both began praying in English, but within minutes the unction of the Spirit overwhelmed us and we were both interceding in the language of the Holy Spirit. Israel yelled to me, "Keep praying! Keep praying in that language! You are praying in the same language the Palestinians speak!"

The prayer continued for about 15 minutes, and gradually the presence of the Lord subsided. I asked Israel, "Did you understand what was being said?" He replied, "Yes I did." Then he proceeded to relate the following:

> You were praying and prophesying about the judgment of God that was soon to come to the earth. But you also spoke about a terrorist attack that would come from this area, and how the terrorist would hide in the rocks of these mountains.

For a brief moment, fear seized me. Was this attack about to happen? Should I scream for the people in the monastery to run down the hill and get on the bus? Israel said, "It is not an attack today, but an attack in the future." When the group returned to the bus, I told a few close friends what happened but didn't tell everyone. I didn't want to cause any unnecessary distress or fear.

A year later we returned to the Holy Land. Israel Acrobauch came to the hotel in Jerusalem to greet the group. He immediately said, "Perry did you hear about the terrorist attack near the monastery?" I replied that I had heard nothing. He began telling me that a Jewish school had carried a group of children to visit the monastery, which is located in the West Bank section of Israel. Halfway into their walk, terrorists hidden on the mountains behind some rocks began shooting at the children. Then the strangest thing happened! As suddenly as it started, the shooting stopped and the terrorists fled in the van.

There could have been a massacre. Instead, something unexplainable must have spooked the terrorists. Israel said, "Perry, the children were standing at the same spot where you and I were praying last year. God marked the spot with your prayers!" In the Old Testament God would mark the spot where men would pray and offer sacrifices. When a man needed to hear from the Lord, he would return to the site of the altar, knowing that God had marked the spot.

The anointed prayer of the Holy Spirit ascended to the throne room of God, and said, "There will be an attack here. Protect those who will walk here." God had watched that site for a year, and prepared a way of escape for the children.

YOU WILL NEED A PLANE

Israel Aerobauch has been used by the Holy Spirit on numerous occasion to confirm a word in season or to give spiritual instruction by the inspiration of the Spirit.

On one occasion my office manager, Charlie Ellis, showed Israel a photograph of a young lady he was dating. Israel began mumbling under his breath, and said, "The Lord said this is the one you will marry." Charlie married her several months later. Years have passed, and today he and Mona have a lovely daughter named Isabella.

In 2001, before the September 11th terrorist attack, Israel was praying and interceding in our hotel suite in Jerusalem. He began predicting, "Perry, you need a small plane of your own to travel to your meetings. The Lord is telling me that you need a plane. Something is going to happen in America that will affect the airline industry and you will need your own plane." I was uninterested in a plane and had no additional income to purchase one. I didn't know a pilot who could fly one.

I returned to the Holy Land in 2002, and Israel said, "Do you have the plane yet?" I said I didn't, and he said, "You're not listening to the Lord. You need a plane now!" After prayer, I found a pilot from my home church who searched for three months, and found a Cessna 421 that we now use to travel to most of our meetings! The plane saves valuable time we once lost waiting in long security lines, spending nights in cities, dealing with security personnel, delays in flight schedules and mechanical problems often encountered with commercial airlines!

Israel operates in the prophetic gift and in the words of wisdom and knowledge. He will often confirm things God has already revealed. These are revelation gifts, revealing secret, hidden things. This is one of the same purposes of the gift of tongues, to speak and reveal the mysteries of God (1 Corinthians 14:2).

Just as Rufus and Dad were both used in the gift of tongues, the same precious gift has manifested on numerous occasions throughout our ministry as both a sign to the unbeliever and as a means of revealing the hidden mysteries of God. Many times, after praying in the Spirit, I will receive inspiration for a message, the words for a new song or a creative idea that becomes a blessing to the ministry.

Transferring the Gifts of the Spirit

Often a person will ask a minister to pray that they will receive the anointing. Once a young minister came to me and asked me to lay hands on him and pray he would receive *my* anointing. I responded, "I will also pray you will receive my attacks, my discouragements and my burdens!" He fired back, "No, I don't want all of that, just the anointing."

First, it is not *my* anointing or *my* gifts; it is the anointing of the Holy Ghost and the gifts of the Spirit. Every believer who is filled with the Holy Spirit already has an unction, an anointing of the Spirit (1 John 2:27).

The flow of the anointing increases with prayer, fasting and the study of the Word. The anointing came on individuals in the Bible when the anointing oil was poured on them (1 Samuel 16:13).

Oil comes from olives and olives must be crushed to obtain the oil. When I see someone who carries a strong anointing, I ask myself, *I wonder what he has been through?* Out of personal times of crisis flows the ointment of the Spirit.

Paul transferred spiritual gifts to Timothy by the "laying on of hands" (2 Timothy 1:6). Paul also called Timothy his "son" (1Timothy 1:2). This personal, intimate relationship between the teacher (Paul) and student (Timothy) qualified Timothy to receive the impartation of gifts from the great apostle Paul.

This father-to-son transfer of spiritual gifts was beautifully illustrated when God called Jesus *My beloved Son* at the Jordan River and "imparted" the fullness of the Holy Spirit upon Christ (Matthew 3:17).

The reason I believe I was a "qualified candidate," even as a teenager, to ask Rufus for prayer and receive the same type of spiritual gifts is because there was a long relationship between him and my father. First, they were related by marriage; and secondly, Dad had traveled with Rufus in his early ministry. The mentor-teacher, father-son relationship is important in the act of impartation.

Every person called into ministry or who desires to be used of God should find someone called of God with the same office of ministry. He should look for a person with a similar gifting and be mentored by this person. It may be impossible to sit under this person's teaching or follow him from place to place, but you can glean from a mentor's personal knowledge, and from any printed or recorded resource material he has produced.

LESSONS I HAVE LEARNED IN THESE EXPERIENCES

- ◆ God puts people in your life to impart their blessings, knowledge and anointing to you.
- ◆ You must be willing to endure trials in order to enjoy the anointing.

- The anointing is for ministry and gifts, not just to feel good.

- You must have a spiritual father or mentor and be a son before you are a leader.

- The gifts can be received, but must be maintained by continual operation.

- A word of knowledge or prophecy often confirms what you are already feeling.

- You will take on the gifts and the similarities of those who mentor you.

CHAPTER 6

AMAZING LOVE—
FINDING MY
LIFE'S PARTNER

He who finds a wife finds a good thing, and obtains favor from the Lord (Proverbs 18:22).

AMAZING LOVE— FINDING MY LIFE'S PARTNER

To receive Christ as Lord and your Savior is the greatest decision you will make in your life. You can live without a lot of material things, but you cannot enter the kingdom of heaven without a relationship with Jesus Christ. The second most important decision you will make will be whom you choose as your lifelong companion and helper (Genesis 2:18).

This is especially true if you are active in ministry. Your spouse makes important emotional, spiritual and physical deposits into your life, and his or her attitude and actions may pull the strength, joy and energy out of your heart. A spouse can make or break you. The person who finds a lifetime soul-mate finds a good thing. But beware of the many counterfeit "loves" you may encounter on your journey to discover God's chosen partner for your life.

MARRYING A PREACHER

When I was preaching revivals throughout Virginia, West Virginia and Maryland in the late 1970s, it was a common occurrence for a mother or dad to invite this "young evangelist" over to their house for dinner. It didn't take long for me to figure out the hidden agenda behind these meals. There was usually a young Christian girl—a daughter, granddaughter, niece or distant female relative—who happened to be single and looking for her "Mrs. Degree."

During those times I enjoyed the food and the spiritual conversations, and returned to my lodging to study and pray for the service. I wasn't interested in playing the dating game. Some of the young girls were emotionally immature and simply wanted to "marry a preacher." Often, it was to live out the dream of a mother or grandmother.

There seemed to be some spiritual or mental fantasy attached to becoming a minister's wife. A minister stands before attentive crowds, giving spiritual truth and usually wearing nice clothes. The mystique of traveling from state to state, seeing new places, meeting new people and eating in different restaurants seemed like a perfect life. A young minister's wife could attend the state camp meetings, the conventions, and the denomination's General Assembly. Perhaps the idea of marrying a minister made a woman feel significant, or spiritually secure. Or perhaps the mother felt that if her dear daughter married a man of God, this would keep her out of trouble! I can assure you that many young women would have been disillusioned and disappointed had they tied the knot with a young, traveling minister.

THE EARLY REVIVALS

In my early ministry, many small rural churches were not spiritually prepared for a revival. Usually a revival was a set time to bring the dedicated members together for a time of spiritual emphasis. During revivals, I often spent hours alone in study and prayer, only to minister to a congregation of believers whose interest in revival peaked decades ago. The early accommodations were sometimes the best they had; at other times, quite embarrassing. I have stayed in small attics and in basements with cold concrete floors, where the restroom and shower were in the church facility. I would have to beat the Sunday School attendees to the men's room in order to prepare for church.

A large church in North Carolina offered me the "Evangelist's Apartment" in the church. This meager room joined the kitchen and the daycare facilities. The "apartment" was furnished with an old couch that served as a sofa bed. The springs were so worn that it dipped about five inches in the center. The rest of the furniture consisted of a TV with rabbit ears, a small table and chairs with wobbly legs, and a small sitting sofa.

Often, I studied until 2 o'clock in the morning, only to be awakened at 6 o'clock by the children coming into the daycare. We stayed in these conditions for four weeks, and had a wonderful revival, despite the fact that the pastor withheld offerings from our ministry and collected funds for his own evangelism fund. Not every woman would endure this lifestyle. The wife must be called of God just like the man. She may love and marry the man, but she must also love and marry his ministry.

YOUR CHOICE OR GOD'S CHOICE

Being a single evangelist held its own set of challenges. If you are single, don't make any sudden uncertain moves, especially in the area of marriage. From age 16 to 19, I met two young women, both Christians, that I thought I would marry. (Yes, I realize that 16 is young, but have you heard of "puppy love"?)

The first young lady was a member of my father's church. A dedicated Christian, she also sang and played the piano, a real plus for any minister. I met her before I was called into the ministry. For my birthday she bought me my first *Dake Annotated Reference Bible*, which I have to this day. Shortly after announcing to her father that I thought I would marry her, her dad's job was transferred out of state, thus stopping cold any opportunity for a future relationship.

At the time this seemed to be a negative event, but it later proved to be the right thing. This young woman would have been my first choice, but not God's choice. As time passed, I recovered from my emotional connection with this girl, and began to concentrate on my unexpected call into the ministry.

Months later, during a church youth camp in Virginia, I met a pastor's daughter who caught my attention. She had dark hair, a friendly personality and she too could play the piano and sing. After inquiring, I found out that she was also a public school teacher. At first I used a mediator to send messages between us, but I finally gained the courage to speak to her. We hit it off quite well; and as time progressed, we developed a close friendship and a personal relationship.

After 18 months of talking on the phone, writing letters and spending time together when possible, I determined that this must be the right person to marry. In December, 1979, we began to discuss the possibilities of marriage. At this time I received an unusual phone call from a fellow minister. The phone call was instrumental in changing my plans for marriage.

The Call from Marcus Lamb

When the call came, I was spending some time at my fiancées house, getting to know her family better. The telephone rang, and my fiancée answered. "Perry, someone named Marcus Lamb wants to talk to you."

I thought, *Marcus must have concluded another great revival and he wants to tell me about it.* We had conversed on many occasions about our revivals and what God was doing. We were both having some of the greatest extended revivals in the denomination at the time. "Hey Marcus," I said in my usual, easygoing tone.

"Perry," Marcus said, cutting to the chase. "I normally wouldn't get involved in something like this but the Lord has really dealt with me about you. There is something I need to tell you."

I didn't know where he was headed in the conversation, but he had my undivided attention.

"You know the girl you are planning to marry?"

"Yes," I said, trying to guard my words from those mingling in the house.

"Well, the Lord has dealt with me strongly" Marcus said, with a tone of warning in his voice. "He has impressed me that it is not His will for you to marry this girl. If you marry her, you will be making a big mistake." I felt my heart pound. Blood rushed to my head. At first I reasoned to myself, *What does Marcus know about this girl or about God's will for my life? I am the one who feels like this is the right thing to do.*

From that moment, I don't remember much of the conversation that followed. I trusted Marcus as a friend, and knew he was used in the gifts of the word of knowledge and the word of wisdom. I wanted to take Marcus' word, but I also needed a confirmation from the Lord, a sort of second opinion on the matter. When I hung up, I never told the young lady what Marcus said. We continued to discuss marriage plans.

THE SECOND CONFIRMATION

A few days later, my fiancée and I were together in the basement of her house, discussing June wedding plans. Since June was only six months away, I was asking God for a confirmation of His will. As the discussion progressed, she suddenly made it clear that she had certain expectations for our future relationship.

She said, "Once we are married I do not want to stay in people's homes. You need to look into purchasing a bus or motor home to travel in." I thought to myself, *I am trying to make a car payment and you want a bus? Dream on!*

She continued, "Since I have a ministry of my own, it is important that I sing at least one or two songs before you preach." I thought to myself, *What if the church has other singers, or if the Holy Spirit moves in another direction?*

After the phone call and this airing of demands, my inner peace was taken from me. At first I thought, *This is just the devil trying to hinder God's will.* Perhaps I needed more confirmation. I have since learned that the presence or absence of inner peace is often your strongest confirmation of God's will.

I have a policy to never move on a major decision until I feel total, inner peace. Inner unrest is a signal to me to stand still and cease from making a major change or decision. When you don't know what to do, it is best to do nothing except stand still and wait on the Lord.

Preaching out of State

In 1979, I was appointed as the youngest State Evangelist in the Church of God in Virginia. As a state-sponsored minister, the board limited the number of times I could preach out-of-state to just two revivals a year. In late 1979, invitations to minister in other states began pouring in. In February 1980, I left Virginia to minister at the Northport Church of God in Alabama. The revival was scheduled for a week.

I knew something special would happen at this church. Three months before, in November, I had dreamed of preaching in a church with a large, square-shaped sanctuary with orange-colored carpet and orange fabric on the pews. In the dream, I walked out of the men's room to a door with a window and peered into the sanctuary. I clearly remember the youth sitting together in the far end of the church and a large choir gathering in the choir loft to sing. I had never seen this church.

When I walked into the Northport church, however, I saw the sanctuary and told the pastor, "I have seen this church before." I pointed down the hall and said, "There is a men's restroom down the hall on the left, and across from the restroom there is a door entering the sanctuary, that has a window. The youth sit over there. He was stunned, and said, "You are right." I said, "We will have the greatest revival in this church's history!"

During the second week of this revival the girl I was engaged to traveled from Virginia to Alabama to attend the meeting. Before preaching I introduced her as my fiancée, and you could almost hear the gasps from the youth group. I had not mentioned I had a "girlfriend," much less a fiancée. After she returned home, many of the youth began whispering among themselves, "She and Perry are not meant for each other."

I began to realize, *Someone is not listening here, and I think it is me!* Several nights later, I was in a pizza restaurant in Northport when I received a phone call from the young woman. I informed her that I didn't understand why but we must break up our engagement. "I just don't feel this is a right decision," I explained. To my surprise she agreed.

When I returned to the crowded room with about 40 youth from the church, I announced I had broken up with my fiancée. Suddenly, applause erupted from the group. "You did the right thing," they said, encouragingly.

THE EVENTS THAT FOLLOWED

I soon learned the truth to the words of the old song, "Breaking Up Is Hard to Do." The emotional ties did not sever easily. The revival was now ending its second week. I was scheduled to close the Northport revival on Saturday night, and begin another revival in Sylacauga on Sunday morning. In my spirit I knew the Northport meeting was not finished. However, I desired to remain true to my commitment.

During the Saturday night altar service, I was in the middle of a long prayer line, ministering one-to-one, when suddenly the

Holy Spirit flashed these words in my spirit, "Did I tell you to close this meeting?" There I was, frozen in one spot, dripping wet with perspiration. Again I heard, "Did I tell you to close this meeting?" I answered back, out loud, "No you did not!"

The inner voice of the Holy Spirit said, "What are you going to do?" My mind began racing, "I need to call Pastor Kennedy in Sylacauga and cancel our revival." I knew if I closed the Northport meeting out I would miss the will of God. I grabbed the microphone and said, "The Lord spoke to me. I need to make a phone call!" Leaving the people in the prayer line and the entire church in limbo, I went to the pastor's study and made the difficult call. Naturally, the pastor in Sylacauga was upset with my decision, but I was determined to fulfill God's purpose.

I returned to the sanctuary and said, "The revival is going on!" Suddenly the glory of the Lord fell on the people, confirming that we were all doing the will of God. Little did I know that the two additional weeks of revival were not just about the revival, but would be about discovering my destiny and the woman God had chosen for me.

THIS IS THE GIRL YOU WILL MARRY

Despite the marvelous move of God, I was still licking my emotional wounds after breaking up with my fiancée. Sitting on the platform during the third week of the revival, something unexpected happened. As the choir was singing, I was observing the worship of the youth group, about 100 strong, sitting to the left of the platform. My attention was drawn to an attractive young lady with long brunette hair flowing down her back. She was dressed in a black skirt, white blouse and black jacket. Her face was glowing like an angel's with the peace of God.

Suddenly, I heard that still, small voice that had spoken to me on other occasions. It said, "This is the girl you will marry!" The voice was real, but unexpected. I immediately fired back, "Get behind me Satan, you won't distract my mind!"

As I thought this, I heard the inner voice say again, 'This is the girl you will marry!" At this point, the Lord had my attention. In a flash I thought, *This must be why the revival went on. I hardly know this girl, but if God says she's the one, then she's the one.* I hid these words in my heart and told no one. I had learned from past experience there are some things you should keep to yourself. Just as Mary "pondered certain things in her heart" (Luke 2:51) concerning Jesus, I hid these words from that moment forward. At that moment I reasoned, "If I'm going to marry her I'd better get to know her during this revival."

I PLANNED MY STRATEGY

After negative experiences in the past, I had made it a policy not to date any girl during a revival. I would go out to fellowship with a group of young people, however, if there were mature leaders in the group. The Northport youth enjoyed eating out after every service! I arranged to always sit next to the beautiful 19-year-old named Pamela Taylor. I remember sitting beside her at the restaurant, and shyly reaching for her hand under the table.

As the revival progressed I knew my feelings for her were more than an emotional flash in the pan. The four-week revival concluded and I prepared to journey back to Virginia to minister at another revival. However, I left part of my heart in Alabama with a young ravishing, southern belle who had become woven into the fabric of my life.

After the long, lonely drive to my next appointment, I arrived exhausted. I had been ministering for 11 consecutive weeks. My mind and heart were with Pamela in Alabama. Her southern accent and personal charm had caused me to swoon, and I was in never-never land. The home girls in Virginia couldn't hold a candle to the one whose nicknames were "Pammy Poo" and "Poo Bear." For years, people have heard me tell this story from my perspective. Now, hear it from the thoughts and feelings of my sweetheart, Pam.

PAM TELLS THE STORY

I remember the announcement well. In January 1980, Pastor Walter Mauldin told the church that a young minister would be conducting a revival. The Northport Church of God was known as a "revival church," but we had been through so much that we certainly needed a spiritual breakthrough.

A few of the young girls in the youth group heard that the minister was a single evangelist. This fact caught their attention, but I was not caught up in the desire to be married, and certainly had no special interest in marrying a minister.

When the evangelist arrived, we were all in for a shock. The pale-skinned, skinny, dark-haired 20-year-old preacher sporting a black suit stunned the church with the anointing he had to preach. During the service he told of a dream he had, in November, 1979, of a church with four sections of pews and orange carpet. God showed him the Northport church in detail, and Perry had told the pastor about the dream.

On the first Sunday, Perry boldly announced, "We are going to have the greatest revival that this church has ever experienced!" Many of the old-timers admired his zeal, but grinned out of the sides of their mouths. That is, until he began to operate in the word of knowledge and began to tell things spoken in a private business meeting that morning that only a few people had heard.

This got the attention of the leadership. And this is when they began to take this 20-year-old seriously. At this time my three sisters and I were living with Charlotte and Jerry Skelton and their two boys, a precious family from the church. As we returned home from church each night, we were amazed at what was happening. I had never sat under any ministry that operated more in the power of the Spirit.

During one service, I saw a young man, Joey Franklin, walk down the aisle with a cast on his leg, leaning on two crutches. As Perry prayed, Joey began shaking under God's power. He felt his ankle was being healed. He shouted across the front of the church without the crutches. He went home and told his dad he was cutting the cast off, he had been healed! He returned the next night without the cast or the crutches.

Before I ever fell in love with the man, I fell in love with his ministry. I admired Perry as a bold, dedicated man of God. As the meeting progressed I had no clue that the Lord had spoken to him about me. That is, until I began to pick up some signals that we women, even as teenagers, can pick up. Like little comments about how nice I looked in that dress. Or when he told me my hair looked "so beautiful." But when he reached for my hand under the table at the restaurant, I knew this could be more than a casual friendship.

One night toward the end of the revival, he requested that I drive him back to the church. I knew he would never be in the car with a female unless other people were with him, so I must admit that I was a little nervous. The rain was pouring down and I was to drop him off at the parsonage near the church.

As the rain beat a romantic melody against the car and the windshield wipers appeared to join the rhythm, he took my right hand in his and said, "On nights like this I wish I were married." My heart almost beat out of my chest!

That night, I told Charlotte how I felt. I said, "I think he really likes me, and I like him too." But as other people began to notice his interest in me, some would say, "Well just don't get your hopes up. After he's left town, you'll be forgotten." Somehow I knew they were wrong.

On the last night of the revival, I stood with about 40 other youth and watched Perry pull out of the restaurant, headed back to Virginia. I thought my heart would break. In fact, we all cried. The four-week revival had resulted in over 100 souls being saved and over 75 being baptized in the Holy Spirit. Many of the converts were among the youth. Several of them now pastor churches and are in full-time ministry. We were in his heart and he was in ours—especially mine! As I stood there, my mind raced back to the service where Perry called me out and had me to sit in a chair. The Lord showed him I had not been baptized in the Holy Spirit. Most people in the church assumed I had been, but he was right. That night I received the gift of the Holy Ghost just as Perry said I would when he saw the vision that afternoon during prayer! I was also baptized in water by Perry during this revival.

I recall going home and saying to Charlotte, "I love him. I can't help it, I love him." Again, a few voices of skepticism said, "Don't get your hopes too high. He may not feel the same way about you." My inner female instinct kicked in and told me that he didn't need to tell me he loved me yet. I knew that when he was around me, he had deep feelings for me.

I graduated from high school in May, 1979, and from then until the revival I had a difficult time finding a job. I made $50 a week taking care of a friend's children, but this was my only income. Shortly after the revival ended, I was called for an interview at the University of Alabama for a secretarial position. It was a positive interview and I felt confident I would get the job.

That night I prayed that if it was God's will for me to work at the university and live in Northport for the rest of my life, then I wanted this job. I never heard from the job interview and never went for another one. Without realizing it, not having this job gave me the freedom I would need to assist Perry in the future.

THE PHONE CALLS THAT FOLLOWED

Within days, Perry's letter arrived in the mail. His first letters were simple, friendly and to the point. He always managed to draw some goofy-looking cartoon character, or put a funny joke on the back of the envelope to make me laugh. I always looked forward to going to the mail box to see if a surprise letter was in the mix. I still have one of the first letters he ever wrote me. It is dated March 10, 1980, and mailed from the Virginia Beach Revival:

Pammy,

Surprise! Guess you weren't expecting to hear from me. Oh well, anyway how is everything? Fine I hope. I am in Virginia Beach, Virginia. We had a good service tonight. Got off to a good start.

Boy, I sure do miss all of you. I don't know why I am like that. I think I am real bad in love with everybody. Now before I forget, tell Jeff and Jeff, Don, Duck, Pam, Shelia, Nancy, Tim, Wendy, Pat, Paula, and the rest of the gang to write. I love them all.

I am about dead, physically. It's now about 1:10, and I have had about seven hours of sleep in two-and-a-half days (sounds like the revival doesn't it)! I really want all of you to stay excited about the Lord. All of us have to make it to heaven.

By the way I miss you a whole lot, too. I miss hearing you say, "Jaaaf" (Jeff). If you will give me your phone number, I will try to call sometime.

Also tell Charlotte, Jerry and Barbra I said howdy. They are great!!

Well, I miss you all, and I love you bunches. Be good, and keep the faith.

Love and Prayers,
Perry Stone, Jr.

I managed to get the telephone number to him, and in a few days the first phone call came.

"How is everyone doing?" he asked. "We're fine," I answered in my finest southern Alabama drawl.

"I sure do miss everyone," he said, like a little boy missing his close friends. "We miss you too," I said, sheepishly.

"Well, when Charlotte and Jerry get in, tell them I called. Tell all the young people how much I love them and I miss them all and for them to all keep the faith." "Okay," I answered. *At least he called*, I thought, hanging up the phone. The conversation wasn't that personal but it was a start. Days passed, the calls became more frequent. The conversations also became longer. More letters followed the calls.

THE SURPRISE I WILL NEVER FORGET

Weeks passed and I didn't see Perry. He had planned a secretive visit without informing me. Only my sisters and the folks we lived with knew of the plan, and they were sworn to secrecy.

On that day, I had just returned from the gym. My hair was straight, and I had on no makeup. I was dressed in a ragged outfit that looked like rejected clothes from a goodwill clothing dumpster. My sisters kept bugging me to "throw on some better clothes, curl my hair and put on a little makeup." I asked them, "Why should I, since it is just us girls and our close friends?" Imagine how embarrassed I was when a car pulled up and Perry popped his head through the door. I thought, *If he likes me after seeing me like this, there must be some real love somewhere!*

Later that evening, we sat together in the living room. He took my hand, looked me in the eyes and said, "I think I love you." After his previous experience he was being more cautious, making sure his desires were in God's will.

"I love you too." I replied. Thus the spark that would ignite the flame of marriage had been struck.

WE ONLY HAD ONE DATE

During the 26 weeks of building our relationship, we only went on one official date—to a steak house in Birmingham! Perry was traveling up to three weeks out of each month from state to state.

Our relationship was built through cards, letters and numerous phone calls. Much of our time together was when he passed through, between meetings, or when I traveled with friends to attend one of his revivals. I knew our feelings were strong and our relationship was serious when he flew me up to his parent's house to meet them. I was a nervous wreck. I had never flown, and had never been away from home like that. I was shy about meeting anyone I didn't know. Perry's family was kind, but his 4-year-old sister kept calling me by the name of Perry's ex-fiancée, telling me how much she missed her! I still have Perry's mother's first letter she wrote after my initial visit:

Dear Pam,

I have been trying for days to get around writing to you and letting you know we really enjoyed having you visit with us over the Holidays. I hope you enjoyed your visit as much as we did having you. I really did miss you after you left. I hope you can get back up and visit again.

Tell the family hello, and we would love to see you all again. I don't really have much news, just wanted to let you know that we enjoyed your visit and you are welcome to come back at any time.

Pray for us and our church. We really need a good red-hot revival. I asked Melanie what she wanted me to tell you, and believe it or not, she asked me to tell you that she misses you and wants you to come back. She said she didn't mean all the mean things she said to you!

Well, take care of yourself, and we hope to see you again before too long.

Love and Prayers,
Juanita

This letter was a real encouragement. Months later, Perry asked me to join him and his family at Grandma and Granddad Bava's house during Christmas week. I was soon to learn that Christmas at the Bava's was as much of a family tradition as lighting the Christmas tree at the White House or watching a 99th rerun of the classic movie, *It's a Wonderful Life*. In this family I found a special closeness and joy that I had missed growing up in a divorced home. These people were a hugging and kissing bunch, and were always expressing love and affection to each other.

I was accepted in the family before we were married. Perry's mom would say, "She's a good one, son, better catch her while you can!" Thus I had an opportunity to bond with the family. At this point they believed Perry was serious, and that marriage was in our future.

Life in Danger

Before our marriage, I remember Perry calling me about an incident that occurred in Virginia. During a revival in Dublin, a young man whose father was an Italian Mafia leader from the northeast, was converted to Christ. They had a house on the lake, and the father did not like Perry "converting his son." While eating at a fast-food restaurant one night, the manager asked, "Is there a Perry Stone here?"

Perry identified himself and took the call. It was the Italian father making serious threats against Perry. Perry contacted the police, and was told that they knew about this man and believed him to be a "hit man," but there was no evidence to convict him. The police watched him closely when he was in the area.

They suggested that Perry should move out of the church basement in Dublin where he was staying during the revival, and go to a friend's house in another town. They told him to not let anyone know his whereabouts. After the revival closed, this letter arrived:

Dear Pam,

Howdy! Well, finally I've settled down where I can write. I am now in Kentucky. We had a great service tonight, and the Lord touched.

I closed at Dublin last night. As far as we know, 35 were saved and filled with the Spirit; 70 were baptized in water and 16 joined the church! PTL! It was great. They wanted it to go on, but God wanted me here. Maybe it was best for now.

Guess what? Someone in Dublin stole my wallet. It had $250 to $300 in it. Also my license, etc. I am driving without a license, and won't be back home until the last of June (it's a long story).

Also, someone told me last night (Saturday) that a hippy in a green (new) Continental with North Carolina tags was looking for me Friday night.

I stayed in Salem Friday night, and whoever it was kept hanging around in Pulaski near the church. No one ever found out who it was, and I don't know who it was. Oh well, probably some dude wanting to kill me!

So I told a couple of dope heads at the restaurant about it (one of them was a backslider), and they said, "If anyone tries to give you a hard time, let us know and we will take them on." Isn't that terrible? So I'm kind of glad I am gone.

Well, Lord willing, I'll try to be in Northport late Monday night or Tuesday. I've got a lot of paperwork to do. See if Charlotte will let me use the typewriter. I have to lay out a bulletin, etc. I will probably try to call on the weekend.

Keep the faith, the fire and the love.

Miss You

Love Perry

P.S. Please keep my throat in your prayers; it's gone.

Letters like this one became common, along with telephone calls and occasional drop-in visits when he was preaching in the area. After 22 months of letters, phone calls and drop-in visits, inspiration struck Perry and he finally gained the assurance that it was not good for him to be alone!

He Pops the Question

It could have been a more romantic setting, but Perry always operates in a realm of sudden inspiration. When the unction strikes him, he is ready to jump out of the boat and begin walking on the water!

We were in his car and he was driving me from his home in Virginia to Alabama. Somewhere between Bristol and Knoxville, Tennessee, on I-75, he asked me if I would marry him. After a long pause of about two seconds, I confirmed that I would be more than happy to marry him.

I wondered why it took so long for him to ask me to be his wife. After proposing, he explained the long waiting period. He was sincerely apprehensive that being married could possibly interfere with his private study and prayer time. For five years he had lived in bedrooms in homes and in hotels, often spending up to 14 hours in prayer, study and research of the scriptures.

When he would pass through on his way to a revival, he seldom ate with me or the family. He was always fasting. Pastor Mildred Blair of Montcalm, West Virginia, said, "Perry preached me a three-week revival when he was 18, and I cannot remember him sitting at the table eating dinner one time in those three weeks!"

He also wanted to make sure that I had a good spirit and was not a nagging, complaining type of person, which he said he "would never live with under any condition." He informed me that sometimes he may want me to stay home, if he went to an important revival, so he could give himself 100 percent to fasting and prayer. Of course, this has never happened once; he cannot stand it when I am not near him!

The inner peace of the Lord finally calmed Perry's inward apprehensions. He knew deep down that he needed me, and I wanted him for my companion.

I immediately set out to get him to dress better. He had hundreds of ties, some with the most ridiculous prints imaginable. One was purple with huge white circles. Others would be an embarrassment to a circus clown. I sent most of them to the local Goodwill store. He would beg me "No, don't take that one. It has such memories." Usually the weirdest ties held his firmest attachments.

Among the things I got rid of was an old white belt he wore with his black suit. I began to shop for some shoes that did not have black duct tape holding them together. It was obvious he was so heavenly minded that he was not paying much attention to what he looked like.

In January 1982, just a few months before our wedding, Perry began a revival in Daisy, Tennessee. It was scheduled for a week, but lasted seven-and-a-half weeks. To this day, we meet people who were saved or whose lives were changed in that meeting. After Daisy, Perry traveled to Montgomery, Alabama, and spent three weeks at a church.

When he announced he was closing the revival to be married, a woman called and told him, "You are missing God's will by getting married. You are supposed to stay longer in Montgomery." We discovered she had a daughter who was interested in "marrying a preacher."

Sorry, but he was already taken!

We both knew the time had come for us to be husband and wife, and begin our journey as one flesh. The phone company enjoyed this period in our lives. Perry's monthly phone bill was more expensive than a 1982 new car payment! Being married would be less expensive! He told me, "If we don't get married and I keep calling you on the phone, I'll be bankrupt in 12 months!"

How Will She Handle Everything?

On Friday April 2, 1982, we were united in marriage at the same church where I met Perry during a four-week revival. Joe E. Edwards, pastor of the prestigious North Cleveland Church of God, performed the wedding ceremony. Perry and Joe had a good laugh when Joe reminded Perry just before walking down the aisle that he had the wrong girl. "Perry, didn't you tell me several years ago about some girl in Virginia that you thought God told you to marry?"

They laughed and Perry said, "Obviously, that was one time it wasn't God speaking to me!" Joe became a close friend, and served for several years on our board of directors. We had no honeymoon, spending our wedding night in Tuscaloosa, Alabama. The following day we drove to Gastonia, North Carolina to begin a three-week revival.

Some close friends were wondering if I would be able to handle the pressures of traveling and of the ministry since I had no experience in either. I believe my past actually assisted my future. Not being from a ministry background, I had no pre-conceived ideas that could breed disappointments if things didn't go my way.

Being from a divorced home and living two years with a church family, I had no physical home I was attached to. Even as a child, I always looked for a friend's house to spend the night in. Even as a child I enjoyed spending time away from home. Some evangelists' wives are so connected to their mother and father that they continually want to return home to the folks or consistently complain about traveling. With me, this was no challenge.

The Apartment

We had planned to move to Virginia, near the Pulaski area, since Perry had many close friends in the region. After much thought and prayer, however, we selected Cleveland, Tennessee, as our home. Perry had preached extended revivals in nearby

Chattanooga (7½ weeks), Dalton, Georgia (5 weeks) and Cleveland (2 weeks), and was well known in the area. We rented a two-bedroom apartment from our friend, Brenda Hughes. One room was filled with boxes and the other was our small bedroom.

Months later my sister, Shelia, moved to Cleveland to work in a local church and help us with the mail and with orders. We were gone about three weeks a month, so we gave her our bedroom, as Perry and I were on the road continually. When we were in town, we took the pillows off of the couch and slept on the floor in the small living room. Shelia eventually moved back to Alabama to marry Jeff Branham.

CHALLENGING THE DENOMINATIONAL BYLAWS

The tax for printing posters and the cost of mailing a monthly newsletter and purchasing cassette tapes and office equipment required us to file for 501(c)(3) status, to help save the ministry money. We knew the denomination frowned on having an organization within the organization and did not want any evangelist to become "bigger than the church." Perry saw a loophole in the official statement (it has since been amended) concerning this subject, however.

The bylaw banned a ministry from incorporating unless it was approved by the General Executive Council, the highest ranking officials within the denomination. If they approved, the Voice of Evangelism could become a non-profit organization without any conflict from church leadership.

Perry immediately began the process of presenting his vision of ministry to the committee. After two years of being placed on the back burner, the minister who married us, Joe Edwards, stepped to the plate and informed the other members, "If we do not work with Perry, he may go into another organization to obtain what he needs to further grow his ministry."

The process required five letters of recommendation, a special procedural form and a report of the yearly income from the ministry—along with a vision statement of its future. After an important discussion, the majority of the committee voted in favor of permitting the Voice of Evangelism to operate as a separate organization within the structure of the denominational organization.

This information was completed for the committee and the legal papers were filed with the state of Tennessee and the U. S. Government. We used a Chattanooga attorney who was responsible for writing the laws for non-profit organizations in Tennessee. On October 18, 1985, less than three months after filing the papers, we were approved, and the Voice of Evangelism became a 501(c)(3) organization! The office in the apartment was too small to store the new books Perry was printing, and soon we were looking for a small house with a basement to house our ministry office.

THIEVES BREAK IN

Eventually, we found a house with three bedrooms and a basement. The basement served as the ministry office. Rick Towe, a businessman who had attended the Daisy meeting, bought us an Apple computer so we could manage our mailing list. Rick had experienced a dream of golden rain falling around him, and accepted it as a sign that God would bless him for supporting our ministry. The basement was soon filled with boxes, tapes, duplicators and ministry brochures.

On the day after Thanksgiving, we pulled into the driveway, having been gone for the week. Perry pressed the garage door opener and yelled, "The side door entering into the garage is open." As we drove into the garage, we saw that the basement door leading into the house had been kicked open. Thieves had broken into our house!

Perry shut off the engine and ran into the house yelling. "I hope you are still here because I am going to break every bone in your body!" I had never seen him angrier. Going through the house, we found that a new video camera, some electronic equipment and a few other items were missing. Drawers were lying on the floor, with the contents scattered.

We were both amazed to discover that the new computer was still in the basement. Had it been stolen, our entire mailing list would have been taken, and we had no backup. The break-in created a feeling that I had been physically violated by a stranger. It took some time for me to recover from the unclean feeling that an intruder had placed his hands on my personal and private "stuff" in my house.

In those days we had no choice but to maintain the ministry office in our home. We didn't have additional money to hire anyone, much less to pay for office rent. Actually, we never really rested when we were at home. Perry would unpack and stay up most of the night, answering mail.

This went on until we found a small 350-square-foot space, which we refurbished and set up for the new office.

We had two employees—Perry and me! When we had our first Pigeon Forge Camp Meeting, we both worked 18 hours a day for three consecutive days, preparing videos, tapes and resource material for the meeting. We were both exhausted before the meeting arrived.

We outgrew this office and eventually located a 2,000-square-foot office in South Cleveland. The cost of the building was $90,000. To us, it may as well have been a million dollars; we didn't have the money. However, we knew how to pray and believe God.

We sent out our first letter, asking friends to donate to our new office. In a short time the need was met and the red brick building was paid in full. This is where Jonathan, our son, spent much time riding his tricycle down the hall, carrying some mail or a video tape to the shipping room in a basket attached to his "three wheeler."

Charlie Ellis came on board as office manager and Perry's brother, Phillip, took charge of the mail room and assisted in tape duplication.

CONTINUAL GROWING PAINS

From 1984, it seemed we had continual growing pains in our ministry. The revivals were averaging three weeks in length, and when we returned home there was so much mail to answer. On one occasion, we were in church for 16 straight weeks! After our first child, Jonathan, was born, I chose to continue traveling with Perry and home school Jonathan.

I can remember standing behind the book table answering questions, selling resource material, duplicating tapes and watching Jonathan in his carrier. Returning home, we went to the office and set up Jonathan's crib in my office. It was a real joy to watch him grow and mature into a fine young man.

ASKING FOR A STRANGE SIGN

After two years, the growth required a new facility to house the operation of our ministry. We searched Cleveland for six months and found nothing. Becoming discouraged, we gave up and said, "God, you find it."

The next week we were eating at Mr. B's Buffet. The owner was planning to move to a larger facility, so while sipping iced tea, Perry asked him, "Is this place for sale?" He answered, "I have an option to buy it, but I'm moving. Would you like to buy my option if the owners say you can?" "I sure would," Perry replied, almost nonchalantly. Mr. B said, "I'll call Mr. Davis right now."

We looked at each other and Perry had this boyish grin. I knew he was thinking, *I just found our building.* Mr. B returned and said, "Mr. Davis said you can buy out my option, but you must do it by January 31." We never make a major decision until we know it is in God's plan. Perry asked the Lord for an unusual sign. At that time we were in a revival in Cleveland, and Perry knew Mr. B had never received the gift of the Holy Ghost. Perry said, "God if I am to purchase that restaurant for the ministry, let Mr. B receive the Holy Ghost in my Cleveland meeting."

The revival at Church of the Harvest in Cleveland passed, and the sign he requested did not transpire. On Monday morning, following the revival, Mr. B closed his restaurant. He set up a meeting to talk to Perry. When Perry arrived, another minister was with Mr. B, discussing the baptism in the Holy Spirit!

Before the meeting ended, Perry and the minister laid hands on Mr. B, and he was instantly filled with the Holy Ghost. He began to speak with other tongues there in the restaurant! He did receive the Baptism in a "meeting in Cleveland," after all!

Perry came home, "It's a go! We are going to get that building!" Five minutes before our option ran out on January 31, we signed papers at the bank for the additional money to purchase the building. The cost was about $275,000, a huge step for a local church evangelistic ministry. We were never reluctant to step out when we knew it was God's will, however. We believe that when God gives the vision, He also releases the provision.

BIRTH PAINS, STAFF PAINS

Years ago the Lord spoke to us about our staff. He said, "Some will be long-term and some will stay short-term. Some, I will send just to be a blessing to you; and some, you to be a blessing to them." Many of our present staff members have been with us for many years, such as Charlie Ellis, and Juanita, Perry's mother. We have experienced our times of "staff infection." An incident I will share taught us a valuable lesson about proper discernment.

A person came on our staff around the mid-1990s, and we began to observe that she was negative in her conversation—and rather outspoken—about certain family members and about her home church and pastor's family. We thought she was venting because of a series of negative personal experiences, and just needed someone to talk to. But Perry pointed out, "She really should not be telling anyone about someone else's personal problems. It is not her business or ours." She became close to me, and my son adored her. During this time, I began to experience the most bizarre mental thoughts of my life. I felt as though something was going to happen to me and I was going to die. It is difficult to explain. It was not an actual fear of death, but an inward feeling that something bad was going to happen and I needed to make preparations for it.

Little did I know that at the same time, Perry had two disturbing dreams. One involved a coffin in a church, and the second dream involved an automobile accident. When I finally told Perry of the strange feeling I was having, he became concerned that a terrible strategy had been planned against me, and we may be receiving advanced warning. As I began to rationalize these feelings, I began to wonder what Perry and Jonathan would do without me? *Perhaps*, I thought, *this young woman who was single could help them in some way.* I eventually thought that this could be the reason she was working with us. Unfortunately, at one point I made the mistake of briefly sharing my thoughts with her.

A few months later, she and Perry had a verbal conflict which caused a rift between them. The Lord arranged for her to meet a fine young man, and they planned their marriage. The week before she left the ministry, however, she called for a meeting with us and two other close friends. She immediately began to criticize Perry, pointing out what she believed were his faults. Prior to this, she had said that God used her to see things in people's lives and expose it. She called this a "ministry of confrontation."

I knew that once Perry was pushed to the limit, his temper would flare up and he could say things he would later regret. I could also see that she was reading her own opinions into situations, and not assessing things with accuracy. Sadly, our friendship was severed and she left in a negative manner.

Wisdom from Karen Wheaton

Months later, I was sharing the feelings I had of death with Rick Towe and his wife, Karen Wheaton Towe. I asked Karen, "Where did this spirit of death come from?" Karen replied, "It is possible that somehow the young woman brought it into your home and ministry. It does not mean she was a bad person, but somewhere there was a spirit of separation and confusion that came into her life." Once she left the ministry, the terrible dreams ceased and the feeling of death immediately departed from me.

We made some important discoveries from this experience. When we hire a person now, we do more than go by what we see and hear. We check with people who knew them personally. We try to hire individuals who know and love us and are not just interested in working in a ministry. When we hire a single, female staffer, Perry wants to know if she has a strong relationship with her family, especially her father if he is living. If a person is married, Perry makes sure the individual has a strong and healthy relationship with the spouse. Negative home relationships bleed over into office relationships. Good family ties produce a positive work ethic.

We recently hired a young lady we have known since she was four. We have preached revivals in her home church for 20 years. We know the family as well as her personal life and dedication to God. We tease her and tell her that if she would wait a few years, we would love to have her for a daughter-in-law! It is important to know those you surround yourself with, and not allow a bad apple to turn you away from the good fruit on the tree.

Why Me?

I have wondered from time to time why God chose me to be Perry Stone's companion. I have told Him that there are so many others who would have been more talented in the area of music or singing, in the area of business administration or in meeting people and dealing with the public. He has always reminded me:

Pam, I didn't need a singer as a wife; I have good singers in the ministry. Nor did I need someone keen in business, because I have that ability, or I could hire staff to fulfill that role.

God knew I needed a wife who would create a peaceful and loving atmosphere in our house. He wanted our home to be a place where our children come running into my arms, and where I can enjoy a home-cooked meal, away from the hectic hours of traveling, flying and eating out. God knew I needed YOU!

Select Your Friends Carefully

If you are a full-time minister with a growing church or ministry, one of your most important decisions will be who connects with your ministry and who you hire on staff. We always remind our staff that they represent us when they are dealing with people. People often see them or speak to them before they speak to us or meet us. Some folks call the office and can be quite obnoxious and quick-tempered. I remind the workers to be as patient as possible with these people. We have a wonderful staff and they do a magnificent job. We love them and they love us. Perry treats them all as they are family.

It is a long road from a local church in Northport, Alabama to a global ministry. We have hit some bumps in the road and encountered many challenges, but we are not finished yet!

Lessons I Have Learned in These Experiences

- ♦ God has the perfect mate for you. Don't marry a frog and expect a prince.
- ♦ God chose you to be you, and not to be someone else or to fit their shoes.
- ♦ Not all strange feelings come from God; they may be "vibes" from someone else.

♦ Not everyone who is with you now will be with you tomorrow . . . but many will.

♦ Don't let the flame of friendship die just because you get burned by some bad candles.

CHAPTER 7

THE TWO BIGGEST ATTACKS OF MY MINISTRY

Therefore we wanted to come to you—even I, Paul, time and again—but Satan hindered us (1 Thessalonians 2:18).

THE TWO BIGGEST ATTACKS OF MY MINISTRY

The anointing attracts attacks from Satan. After David was anointed to be king, Saul became jealous and made many attempts to kill him (1 Samuel 18:10).

When Christ was anointed by the Holy Spirit, he was immediately led into the wilderness to be tempted by the devil (Matthew 4:1). After Paul's conversion, men in Damascus vowed to assassinate him (Acts 9:23-25).

The anointing is a wonderful and powerful weapon against the kingdom of darkness, and a true revival of repentance is the greatest threat to the Enemy. The Adversary will not sit idly by when the Spirit of God is active in a community of believers. Pam and I discovered this sometimes painful truth from the early days of our ministry.

The Most Bizarre Attack I Ever Witnessed

This story developed over a period of 10 years from the time of the attack to the time Pam and I discovered what had actually happened. It reveals the sly, subtle and sudden strategy of the Enemy and how Satan uses people to fulfill his purposes, even in the church. Warnings often precede major attacks; however, we must be able to discern the warning or we may be caught off guard.

A Warning in a Dream

In the summer of 1981, I had a warning dream. I was standing at the bank of a large lake of clear, blue water, with a long fishing pole in my hands. In a flash, a strong fish seized the bait. As I lifted the rod, I saw the largest fish I had ever caught. Reeling the fish to shore and taking it in my hands, I watched as it suddenly turned into a large serpent.

I threw the serpent on the ground. When I did, it rose up and bit me. I recalled thinking, "This snake bite is going to kill me." I heard a voice saying, "The snake will bite you, but it will not kill you." I threw the snake back toward the center of the lake and it became a fish again. I knew I would return to this lake one day and catch that fish again.

> I realized a snake dream always meant severe trouble or a trial. The fish represented souls and the large lake, a large church or congregation of believers. Several months passed, however, and nothing negative happened. The warning dream faded from my mind.

A Satanic Agent on Assignment

I began a revival in Virginia in the late fall of that year. It was in a large church, and I had many personal friends and converts in the area. The revival was scheduled for a week, but because of the spiritual results it was extended into the second week. I always stayed up late to study and pray, so the pastor suggested I stay in the evangelist's apartment located next to his office in the back of the church. The apartment had no television, no telephone and no way of communicating with the outside. It was well furnished, but at night it seemed you could hear every noise. I kept the bathroom light on across the hall from the bedroom, in case I needed to get up during the night.

One night at 3 o'clock in the morning, I was awakened by the noise of someone trying to get into the church through the back door at the end of the hallway. At first I thought it was the janitor, coming to clean the sanctuary late at night. I heard the doors slam, and knew that someone was in the building. Soon I heard the closet door to the janitorial supplies, located near the apartment, open and close.

In a few seconds someone was at the apartment door, jiggling the handle to the door. I sat up, thinking the pastor was coming to bring some news or relate an emergency situation. I was somewhat agitated that he would not knock, but would come directly into the apartment without an invitation! As the door opened, I sat up to see who the unexpected intruder was.

Fear paralyzed my body when I saw the intruder was not a person I recognized, and was not even human. I could see a creature between the bedroom and bathroom doors that was about four feet high with dull gray-looking skin. Its body appeared to be wrapped in old cloth, reminiscent of the Egyptian mummies buried in the tombs of Egypt.

The creature was wearing a pair of old overalls, so filthy that they looked like something pulled from a dumpster or garbage can. It was carrying what appeared to be two bags of garbage, one over each shoulder. I lay back down, pulling the cover up to my neck, foolishly hoping it would not see me! I literally pinched myself to see if this was a dream, but I was completely awake.

I could hear the "thing" throwing trash throughout the apartment kitchen. Moments later, it walked past me without any garbage and peered into the bedroom, still laughing. I pretended not to see it. The creature then exited the apartment, slamming the door as it departed. This was not a dream. I was literally seeing activity involving some form of unclean spirit.

It was as though my hearing was magnified as I heard the creature enter the pastor's offices next to the apartment. Oddly, the creature was opening and closing the pastor's filing cabinets. Minutes passed, and the unclean spirit made its way up the stairs to an area the church used for a kitchen and for the pastor's council room. I never heard it leave this area. After praying under my breath for some time, I managed to fall asleep.

I was hesitant to tell anyone what had happened. I felt they would consider it all a figment of my imagination, or just a wild "evangelistic" story. I was unaware that this spirit was an invisible, assigned agent of Satan and was planning a major attack against this church, the pastor and my ministry.

The revival continued, and the crowds grew until we could not seat people in the building. Countless hundreds were being saved and filled with the Spirit. We would later learn that the selling of drugs almost ceased in several surrounding counties as hundreds of youth from the local high school were spiritually stirred and saved.

Altar services would last into the night and prayer meetings were breaking out throughout the sanctuary. The revival had the attention of heaven, but it also had the attention of the powers of darkness.

The Revival Was Suddenly Closed

I had preached several revivals at this church, and considered the pastor a friend. We had never had a disagreement, although he never understood the various manifestations of the Spirit that were occurring in the services. In the third week of the revival, he gave a directive for the sanctuary doors to be locked before 11 o'clock. This prevented prayer or intercession from occurring in the church. He then began discussing closing the meeting down because he and his wife were tired and they had planned a vacation. Another speaker was scheduled, and he implied that some were threatening to quit coming to church if he didn't "take control" of the meeting.

The meeting lasted four-and-a-half weeks, and was closed on Wednesday night with an overflow crowd and over 20 people receiving the Holy Spirit. During the altar service, several of the elders went to ask the pastor if he would take his vacation and allow the meeting to go on under their supervision. The pastor had already made his way home.

For some reason, it appeared, he didn't want the meeting to continue, and no one knew why. In the altar service I made the mistake of telling the congregation, "I may get in my car and go back to Alabama tomorrow, but I will be out of God's will doing it." My frustration was legitimate but my comments were inappropriate, because it appeared I was contradicting the pastor's decision to close the revival.

I left the next morning, grieved that such a great meeting was closed so suddenly without a legitimate reason. When the pastor returned from a brief Thanksgiving vacation four days later, he was met by some members who wanted an explanation for why the revival was not extended. He said, "If you knew what I knew, you would have done the same thing."

Immediately, speculation swirled throughout the church, and people asked, "What does the pastor know that we don't know?" Others said, "Something must have been going on that was wrong." Out of frustration, the pastor made a comment about the revival during his message that morning. It was broadcast throughout the town on the radio program.

When the service concluded, several unsaved husbands who listened to the service at home told their wives, "You're not going back there. That preacher said some things I didn't like." This only added to the confusion.

THE MEETING THAT TOOK A WRONG TURN

A few days later the state overseer of the denomination came to the church for a brief revival. Several church leaders requested a meeting to discuss the controversy. It appeared that some desired a pastoral change, and others wanted to speak out against the revival. Instead, he met only with the elders, or the pastor's council.

Later, when the overseer did meet with the congregation, he allowed anyone to "stand up and speak your mind." The meeting began with the overseer and pastor blaming the revival for the confusion.

Ethically and legally, my name should have never been brought up in this public setting without me being present to answer the questions. Several friends present stood to defend the great revival. The overseer also permitted the people to clap if they agreed with a certain side. This pitted people against people, especially when folks clapped for a certain view.

Another error was made, in my judgment, when the overseer allowed women to speak their minds. This was a mistake because under these circumstances, it was easy for a woman holding an emotional grudge against another woman to speak up. Some who spoke up and took opposing sides held bitter feelings for years after this one meeting!

In wisdom, the church's sound engineer taped the entire meeting and sent me the cassette tape to hear what was discussed. He did this so I would not hear reports based on rumors.

As I listened to the tape, I could not believe my ears. No one recognized this as a Satanic attack. Not one person stood and said, "This is an attack from the Enemy. We need to pray!"

Instead, it was the revival crowd against the anti-revival crowd, the pastor's friends against Perry's friends and the people who wanted a change in leadership against those who didn't. The meeting left more confusion than any other part of the conflict.

THE RUMORS BEGIN TO FLY

Such confusion always breeds unfounded rumors. Within a month, lies were being circulated about me that spread faster than the winter flu. A minister claimed that while ministering in Alabama, I had hit the pastor in church, then jumped up and told the congregation I was starting a new church in the area.

Someone else repeated the lie that I was banned from ever preaching in Virginia. Another rumor said that I had moral problems, and the pastor had to close the revival. Some ministers began saying, "We knew Stone wouldn't last. His ministry was growing too fast, and God is knocking him down a notch or two."

In December, I went to the overseer who conducted the meeting and asked him to let me meet with the pastor. If I needed to, I told him, I would apologize to the church. He told me that this was not necessary and that the pastor was physically sick. He said he would be moving the pastor to a town where he had a home and could minister and retire there.

Although the overseer told me these things, he changed his story later on. In a major leadership meeting he was asked about the incident in Virginia, and he pinned the blame on me. Some believe the overseer did this to ensure that nothing negative would be connected to his name. This would assure him another leadership position in another state.

My father knew that the lies and rumors were causing people to question my personal integrity. In January 1982, Dad made a personal call to the same overseer and told him that if he didn't personally intervene to stop the lies that were spreading throughout the state, he would carry his church board to Cleveland, along with a lawyer, and bring a slander lawsuit against those who were repeating the lies.

Of course no one, including myself, wanted this matter to go that far, but if you have never been in this type of situation, you don't know what you would do to preserve your good name.

In the same month, January, I requested a visit with Dr. T.L. Lowery who was a member of the executive committee. He advised me, "Perry, you are a young man with a great future of ministry. Leave the situation alone and let the Lord avenge you. One day the very people who are persecuting you and speaking against you will come out to hear you preach."

During this time I discovered how people treat you when they hear negative information about you. I also discovered I had far fewer true friends than I thought. Some pastors began canceling meetings with me, making lame excuses for the cancellations.

Nine months later I attended the General Conference of the denomination where thousands of ministers were registered. During the entire week, men I knew personally would walk past me, ignoring my presence and not speaking to me. Only one minister, Paul Henson, spoke to me, "Perry, I appreciate the great work you are doing. Don't get discouraged, just keep going."

The dream from August 1981, was now clear. The lake was the large church and the fish were the result of the revival. Just when we were about to bring in the catch of souls, the Enemy showed up and bit me in the feet (this represented the carrying of the gospel). I remembered the words, "The snake will bite, but it will not kill you!" At the time I thought, "This may not kill me, but I feel like I'm dying a slow death!"

Losing the Anointing

For several weeks after the meeting I felt I was my only defender. Everywhere I went, I talked about the conflict and the vicious rumors. I knew that if my good reputation and name were ruined, it would be impossible to get them back. I knew I would survive, but felt my survival depended on building my own case against the pastor's attitude and the overseer's.

As I began the process of building myself up, the anointing of the Holy Spirit began departing from me.

In December 1981, during a Sunday morning service in Birmingham, Alabama, I preached without one ounce of the anointing. Closing my Bible and stepping off the platform, I headed to the pastor's office and threw my Bible on the desk. The resentment was building, and I was now beginning to wish harm on those who were lying about me.

A co-laborer named Monty Franklin followed me into the office looking as pale as a ghost. "What is going on? I have never seen you preach, and just walk away without an altar call!" At that moment a precious woman, Ruby Blackwood, asked to see me, and gave me this word, "I don't know what's going on, but the Lord gave me a word for you from Psalms 63:11, 'The mouth of those who speak lies shall be stopped.'"

This was a strong, spiritual woman, and I knew she was led by the Spirit. She gave me my first good news in weeks. This simple *rhema* word kept me clinging to hope. But I needed for God to change my heart and stop the bitterness or I was headed for deep, dark waters. That Christmas at my grandparent's house was the only Christmas in my life where I had no joy of the Lord in my spirit for the season.

GOD BLESSES THREE REVIVALS IN A ROW

Two months after this incident, my schedule took me to Daisy, Tennessee. It was the dead of winter and the church seemed uninterested in revival. On Monday night we canceled the service because of snow, but a carload of kids from Lee College in Cleveland were caught in the snow storm and managed to arrive at 7:30. We went to the church to pray. I told them about the attack I was under and how I needed for God to intervene.

During the prayer meeting, I dragged my carcass around the church, complaining to God. Then I heard the Lord say, "Quit feeling sorry for yourself and think about how big I am." I began to preach to myself about how big God is, recalling every description

I knew from the Bible. Minutes later, Faith, a girl who was play-ing the piano, stopped playing and gave a message in tongues. It was interpreted by another young person, and the Spirit said He had seen what I had been through and was going to send the greatest revival in that church I had ever seen.

I thought, *Nice try friend, but you sure missed that interpretation. Even Jesus himself couldn't have a revival with these folks.* I re-pented for my unbelief three nights later as the church filled up.

For eight weeks we encountered one of the most awesome out-pourings of God that region of the country had experienced in many years. Often, there was standing-room only. People would come three hours early to secure a seat. Over 450 were con-verted to Christ and 550 were filled with the Holy Spirit! Numer-ous miracles happened, and several teenagers who were touched in the revival are now pastoring great churches.

From that meeting I went to Montgomery, Alabama, for three weeks, and on to Gastonia, North Carolina, for a meeting which also lasted for three weeks. Little did I realize that this was God's way of avenging my name and my integrity. Eventually, some ministers reasoned, "Something is not adding up here. If Perry is not anointed by the Lord, then why is he experiencing the fruit and results he is seeing?"

A Meeting with the Pastor

Eight months passed and summer arrived. Pam and I attended the state camp meeting in Virginia. This gave me an opportunity to speak personally with the pastor of the church where the con-flict had risen. He had moved to the very town where, during the revival, he had told me he wanted to retire.

I approached him and began to express my regrets about ev-erything that had happened. I received a cold response. I told him that if he felt I had done something wrong, I wanted to apologize for it. I am sad to say he was unreceptive to my words. After a few comments more, I walked off the platform, knowing I had done according to the Word of God. I told Pam, "I have done all I know to do to make things right." But I was still confused about what all of this meant.

THE TRUTH, TEN YEARS LATER

For 10 years I never knew why the meeting was closed. I felt the pastor was misinformed or pressured by someone or something and made a decision based on those assumptions, but I never had an answer.

Ten years later Pam and I returned to the area to conduct a regional meeting at the Pentecostal Holiness Campground, in Dublin, Virginia. We received a call where we were staying from a young man who had been converted in the revival, but had left the church during the confusion. He had been in a serious car accident, and was requesting for me to come and pray for him in the hospital.

A friend, Alex Wolfe, and I went to his room, and the young man expressed a desire to get right with God. As we prayed the power of God began to shake his entire body. We left the fellow praising God in the bed. Two nights later we were amazed to see him in the revival. He told me he had some important information about the revival 10 years ago, and suggested we go out to eat after church so he could share it with me.

Pam and I, plus five other witnesses, heard the most bizarre story of spiritual warfare we had ever heard. Sipping iced tea and eating pizza, he spoke of the meeting as though it just happened: "Perry, my entire family was saved in that meeting. But when I saw Christians acting against each other, it was too much. I turned on God."

"What did you do?" I inquired.

"Well, I quit the church and eventually became involved with a group that was into Satanism and the occult. Some attended the local university. At first, it was like a game; then it got deeper. We burned candles and did incantations to cause demons to manifest themselves. There were some very high people in the group." He named a few.

I asked him, "So how does all of this fit in with the revival we had in the area?"

"I found out why the pastor closed the meeting and why there was so much confusion," he continued. "One of the men in the church was committing adultery with an occult leader's wife. The leader told the fellow he didn't mind him messing around with his wife as long as he would help shut down the revival."

The revival was hindering the flow of drugs in the area, and many kids from the university were being saved. The drug dealers were angry because of the number of conversions. So it was all about drugs.

I asked, "How could a member shut down the meeting?"

"This particular man who worked the night shift would come by the church on his way to work," he said. "This man reported to the pastor, falsely, that certain things were going on. He even told him you had people coming in and out of your apartment all night long—including women."

I suddenly remembered this man going into the pastor's office and closing the door on at least three separate occasions. The story about women was a lie, because I never allowed women in my apartment. Even when the janitor cleaned my apartment during the day, I would step out. Many youths were praying in the church, but there was always adult supervision.

He continued, "This is the man who helped spread the rumors and lies, not only to the pastor but throughout the town. These rumors and lies about you caused the pastor to close the revival." The young man continued to shock us with the rest of the story.

"When I was involved with this group, I met a young man who was connected with Anton LaVey, the founder of the Church of

Satan. His job was to recruit students from the university into their group. He became aware of your revival, and attended a few nights. On one occasion he told me he knew you were staying in the church, and one night while service was going on, he walked the halls, cursing you. He said he had assigned a spirit to take charge of disrupting the meeting through confusion."

Up to this point one could say he was making up a rather elaborate explanation of past events. His next few sentences, however, sent chills up my back.

"I can give you a description of this spirit. It was about four-foot-high, and was grey in color. If you could see it, it would look like an old mummy."

I almost fell off my seat. To my knowledge I had never related this incident in public in that area. I had told it to only a handful of personal friends, most of whom were sitting at the table. We all stared at each other. This explained how the evil spirit gained access into the church, and why it came into the apartment. It was obvious that the garbage carried by this spirit represented gossip and rumors that fueled the confusion.

The spirit went into the pastor's study. This is where this man was meeting with the pastor, spreading his own lies. The spirit went to the council room. This is where the decisions are made concerning the future of the church. The evil spirit gained access because of strife, confusion and unforgiveness, in the same manner an evil spirit began controlling Saul because of his jealousy toward David (1 Samuel 18:8-12).

At this point the young man said something I will never forget. "That spirit is still connected to that place and will not leave until there is forgiveness and repentance among those who have strife against each other!"

Finally I began to understand why the pastor reacted as he did. If I had been he and I believed the report of this fellow, I may have done the same thing, thinking I was protecting the church.

I had forgiven people a long time ago, but now I understood *why* there was such a reaction. After hearing this, we all agreed that in God's time this should be told to the congregation to clear up any questions people may still have about the issue.

TIME TO MAKE THE STORY PUBLIC

During a 24-year period I returned to minister in this same church about four times under three different pastors. I never shared the entire details of this event until a three-night meeting in May 2004.

During the Sunday night service I was impressed to open my heart and give the minute details of the event. This included the information on the member (without using names), who had started the rumors, and how the unclean spirit was the agent used to disrupt the meeting.

That night concluded in one of the greatest physical and emotional healing services Pam and I have ever witnessed. As forgiveness and spiritual understanding was released, the Holy Spirit confirmed his blessing on us and on the church.

I learned several hard lessons from this trying experience:

◆ Never disagree in public with the person who is in spiritual authority over you.

◆ Never allow strife to continue. Go to the person directly involved in the strife, before it gets out of hand.

◆ Never call a fellow believer an enemy. Just say that there is a disagreement.

◆ All confusion is of the flesh or caused by a wrong spirit, and is never from God.

◆ Attacks may come through people, but the root cause may be a spirit on assignment

◆ Only repentance and forgivness can release you from the power of the attack.

A NEW LEVEL AND A NEW DEVIL

Once the enemy knows he cannot defeat you in one area, he will plan a strategy from another angle. About 10 years after this major attack, our ministry was experiencing a surge of growth. We were producing a monthly magazine, preparing and supplying a monthly tape club, duplicating cassettes and videos, sending out orders for resource material, answering questions in the personal mail and traveling up to three weeks out of a month.

We had four full-time workers: Pam, Charlie Ellis, my brother Phillip, and I. The income to hire people was limited, and the lack of office help created the need for me to put in as many as 18 straight hours of work a day at the office. At this time one of our closest ministry friends, a female teacher, fell into a moral failure that caused great sorrow to Pam and me.

We were close to the entire family and did not know all that happened, but we learned that she was separating from her husband and having a child with another man, whom she married. I knew her as a dedicated, praying woman who spent a lot of time in fasting and spiritual preparation before ministering. Her ex-husband later told me, "I think she spent time preparing to minister to others but did not take time to minister to herself. She was caught in a trap."

About this time my precious son was born, and Pam was recovering. She was getting up early, waking me from my limited sleep in the process. I became tired in spirit and mind. For the first time, Pam and I began to argue over silly things. I remember becoming so angry that I blurted out a rebuke to Pam, causing her to cry convulsively. She was hurt to the core of her being.

During this time a dark cloud of depression and oppression settled over my mind. Dad's mother had experienced a complete nervous breakdown and one of his sisters had struggled with depression. Years ago, Pam's mother had a similar experience. The Adversary knew that depression was something "in the lineage."

As the oppression thickened, the desire to study the Bible, to pray, to answer the mail and to minister was drifting away. I knew I loved my wife and adored my son, but it was as though I wanted to escape all the burdens and responsibilities I was under.

Some would call this a midlife crisis, but my age didn't signify midlife. Others would say I was experiencing burnout, probably the best description of the conflict. Joy was no longer in my life, and I was living on adrenaline and a busy schedule. This was a dangerous place to be, but I continued to function, mostly out of obligation. The grace of God was still working through the meetings as souls were being saved and touched. I could sense the presence of God when ministering, but once I left the pulpit that strange feeling of emptiness came.

The Prophecy from Romania

One evening while alone, I remembered a 12-month-old prophecy from a woman in Romania. During my second trip to Romania, a woman approached me and said,

> I have prayed for you for over a year. One day I heard a powerful spirit talking about how it hated you and wanted you destroyed. Your preaching had shaken up some of these lesser spirits in towns, and they were asking a bigger prince to try to take you down. Be careful and stay before God because you are targeted for a future attack.

I was actually hoping for a word like, "Thus saith the Lord, I am with you, I will bless you, and you will have great success." What concerned me the most was when the Romanian Christians say God spoke to them, they have an impeccable reputation for accuracy. Leaving this church, we traveled several hours to minister in another one.

After the altar service, a woman dressed in traditional orthodox black asked to speak with me. Using an interpreter she said,

"The Lord gave me a revelation. There is a strong spirit that will attempt to attack you, to dirty your hands in order to shut your mouth from preaching the gospel." Her face was stern, yet it expressed concern.

I went to the van thinking, "Why can't I get a *good* word?" not realizing that God was giving me these advanced warnings to prepare me, not to scare me. Now, 12 months later, I was experiencing dark emotions and oppression that I had never experienced. During this time frame I traveled with a group to Bulgaria, on an overseas mission trip. My roommate was international missionary evangelist Rusty Domingue.

On the third night of the trip I awoke and saw a fierce spirit-being hovering over my bed. The creature had long, wiry hair and wrinkled skin. Its eyes were glazed as they glowed with a red tint. After about three seconds, the apparition vanished in thin air.

In retrospect, I believe my spiritual eyes were opened to the type of spirit power I was dealing with. I had recently taught a series called "New Levels, New Devils." The main point of the message is that when we enter a new level of ministry, we encounter a new type of spirit or a new type of spiritual warfare. Our ministry was entering a new arena of overseas missions, in former Communist nations. We were entering an unknown zone that was far different from the average spiritual warfare in America.

During this Bulgarian trip, a friend and I began to write songs. The first song, *Close to the Cross, Far from the Blood* was recorded in 2001 by the Southern Gospel group, The McKameys. This gift of songwriting was somehow in my DNA, but had never been tapped until this crucial time.

Since I am an extremist in everything I do, I became consumed with song writing. Soon I formed a music publishing company, and began planning our first album project.

All the time I was ignoring the needs of my wife and son, concentrating only on myself and struggling with my emotions. My time became consumed with writing songs over the phone. I was reaching out for something new and exciting. I could sense I was disconnecting with my family and my first love of evangelism.

EXPOSING THE DARKNESS TO THE LIGHT

I had to do something. Pam knew something was wrong, but felt helpless, not knowing what to do. We continued to travel and minister. In July, a large tent was erected in Anniston, Alabama. The meeting entered its second week, and I was miserable. One night I stopped preaching and said I had a confession to make.

I began to explain that for two months I had been oppressed and depressed in my mind. I went into as much detail as possible without getting too personal. I gave the invitation and as I was preparing to exit the tent, a small group of friends stopped me.

"Where do you think you are going," they asked.

"I've got to get out of these damp clothes," I said, trying to rush out.

"You're not going anywhere just yet," they said. "You told us what the Enemy was trying to do, and you think we are going to sit back and let him have his way?" one person demanded. "Give me your Bible and notebook, and stand there while we pray."

Someone grabbed a bottle of anointing oil. They began to pray with such volume, it seemed to shake the ground. I felt anointing oil dripping like water over my head and down my face. Then hands were all over my head as my "perfect" hair was beginning to look like a wig being washed at the local beauty salon. Dust was building in the atmosphere around us as they stomped their feet in the sawdust, demanding the Adversary to "get his hands off of God's property." It was a moment of inspiration mixed with perspiration.

I thought, *I wonder what the Lord thinks about this wild bunch?* Suddenly I started laughing out loud, imagining how the Lord was looking down on this dignified preacher, saying, "You needed this!"

When the shouting subsided I looked around and everyone was staring directly at me, as if to say, "Are you free yet?" We started laughing, and I walked up the hill to the pastor's office, covered with oil and sawdust. As I stood looking into a large mirror, I felt a sense of relief. It was not a total deliverance, but a sense of relief that I would recover from this mental assault.

I walked to the car with Pam. Our dear friend, Faye Mims, stopped me and said, "You did the right thing. The Enemy can't hide any more, because you exposed him tonight." Her simple words were a revelation to my spirit. I immediately realized part of the problem. I was fighting a spiritual battle in my own strength, thinking that if I just held on and kept fighting, the Enemy would eventually go away.

This is like hoping a group of terrorists will suddenly change their minds and not attack any more. The way to defeat a terrorist is to expose his plans in advance! When darkness is exposed to the light, the darkness is overcome! Keeping my emotional conflicts and feelings to myself was a huge mistake. As long as I hid them, the Enemy could lurk in the darkness and hide.

When no one knew what I was experiencing, the Enemy laughed and said, "He's too proud to tell anyone what he's going through." Publicly that night, before 800 people, I told them I was struggling for victory over a mental depression. The enemy was now naked before the truth.

In retrospect, my greatest mistake was not sitting down with my wife and telling her how I was feeling. I was leaving her to guess why I was acting in the manner I was. During this meeting the Holy Spirit inspired me with a scripture that I applied to my relationship with Pam:

> Do not forsake her, and she will preserve you; love
> her, and she will keep you (Proverbs 4:6).

God gave me Pam to be a helpmate, and I had ignored one of the most important principles of the Bible. When a man and woman are joined in holy matrimony, the two become one flesh (Genesis 2:24). One can chase a thousand, but two can chase ten thousand (Deuteronomy 32:30). By fighting this battle alone, I was unknowingly cutting the spiritual authority in my life in half. If two become a single unit, then one is only half a unit.

My blessings should be her blessings, but my battles must also be her battles. I determined to open up to Pam and let her know what I was going through. She told me, "Why didn't you say something? You never told me."

The second best decision we made was to go on our first cruise. We took little Jonathan and spent a week on a large boat, just eating, sightseeing, sleeping and lying in the sun. We needed the break from people and ministry. It was the first time in years I had not picked up a telephone, turned on a computer or spent hours in a book or a notebook. Just as Jesus needed to come apart from the ministry, so we must do likewise.

Tell the Devil, "Stone Is Back"

At this time the reality of my mortality struck me. My time was being consumed with ministering to people. The magazine *must* be on time, and the tape club can *never* be late. Every piece of mail must be answered *immediately*.

I suddenly realized that if the Lord tarried, I would die; and in a few years another minister would arrive like a whirlwind on the scene. My magazines would be thrown in the trash and my books placed in the attic with the other junk. The videos and cassettes would be sold for almost nothing in yard sales, and my name would be remembered only by those whom I had touched.

On that ship I realized that my greatest earthly prizes were my child and my wife. My greatest relationships were those of my immediate family and my greatest friends were those who stuck with me through good times and bad times. At that moment I made up my mind to enjoy life with my family. Sure, there are

WILLIAM AND NALVA STONE WITH THEIR SON, FRED—SEPTEMBER 1977.

FRED STONE'S BIRTHPLACE, WHERE THE MIDWIFE ATTEMPTED TO KIDNAP HIM AT BIRTH.

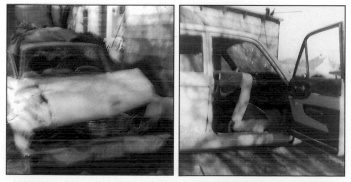

AFTERMATH OF THE CAR ACCIDENT IN 1961 THAT COULD HAVE TAKEN OUR LIVES.
JUANITA'S HEAD WENT THROUGH THE WINDSHIELD AND HER JAW WAS BROKEN.
PERRY JR. WAS THROWN TO THE FLOOR OF THE FRONT SEAT.

R.L. REXRODE AND FAMILY PREPARING TO SING AT AN OUTDOOR "BUSH ARBOR" MEETING.

JOHN AND LUCY BAVA PREPARING TO SING ON THE RADIO.
THEIR DAUGHTERS, JUANITA AND JANET, ARE PICTURED IN THE BACK ROW.

JOHN BAVA (LEFT) AND HIS FATHER, PETE.

FRED STONE (LEFT) WITH LLOYD ADDAIR.
BOTH HAD JUST BEEN CALLED TO PREACH.

FRED AND JUANITA STONE WERE MARRIED ON JULY 9, 1955.

THE FUNERAL OF BABY KENNY EDGAR.
WILLIAM STONE IS BEHIND THE CASKET AND RUFUS DUNFORD IS ON THE FAR RIGHT.

ON OUR WAY TO CHURCH AT BIG STONE GAP, VIRGINIA, 1964.

PAM TAYLOR (MIDDLE)
WITH HER SISTERS, CARLA AND SHEILA.

FORMER CIA AGENT BILL HALL (FAR LEFT) TOLD
FRED STONE UNUSUAL DETAILS ABOUT THE
WATERGATE SCANDAL IN WASHINGTON, D.C.

CAMPMEETING UNDER THE TABERNACLE WAS A YEARLY HIGHLIGHT.
PERRY WAS FILLED WITH THE SPIRIT AT AGE 11 DURING A YOUTH CAMP IN ROANOKE, VA.

THE FOUR-WEEK REVIVAL IN NORTHPORT, AL WHERE PERRY MET HIS FUTURE WIFE, PAM TAYLOR.

THE SUMMER YOUTH CAMP IN VIRGINIA WAS A
HIGHLIGHT OF OUR YEAR AS PREACHER'S KIDS!

PERRY (RIGHT) WITH TIM NUCKLES
IN SALEM, VIRGINIA.

A PHOTO OF PERRY'S PRAYER ALTAR, BUILT BEHIND THE CHURCH CAMPGROUND IN ROANOKE, VA.

AT AGE 18, PERRY SPENT TIME ON THE MOUNTAIN, PRAYING AND READING THE BIBLE.

RUFUS AND MAMIE DUNFORD.
RUFUS PRAYED FOR PERRY
THREE MONTHS BEFORE HE DIED.

THE PEOPLE WHO WERE SAVED AND
FILLED WITH THE SPIRIT DURING THE
11-WEEK REVIVAL IN LAFOLLETTE, TN.

DR. SPENCE AND HIS WIFE, MARY ANN. DAD SPOKE TO HER IN GERMAN THROUGH THE SPIRITUAL GIFT OF TONGUES.

THE 4 ½ WEEK VIRGINIA REVIVAL IN 1981 SAW OVER 100 PEOPLE SAVED.

THE YOUTH GROUP FROM NORTHPORT, AL.
A YOUNG PAM TAYLOR (AGE 18)
IS THIRD FROM RIGHT IN THE PHOTO.

PAM'S FIRST VISIT HOME TO SALEM, VA TO
MEET PERRY'S PARENTS.

APRIL 2, 1982. PERRY & PAM WERE MARRIED AT THE CHURCH WHERE THEY MET DURING A FOUR WEEK REVIVAL.

APRIL 2, 1983 IN WINTER HAVEN, FL. PERRY AND PAM ON THEIR FIRST ANNIVERSARY.

THE VOE QUICKLY OUTGREW THIS 2,500 SQUARE FOOT BUILDING, ITS THIRD OFFICE IN CLEVELAND.

"MR. B" OWNED THE RESTAURANT BUILDING WHICH THE VOE PURCHASED FOR ITS FOURTH OFFICE.
HE IS STANDING WHERE THE VIDEO RECORDING STUDIO WOULD BE BUILT.

PROUD PARENTS AND GRANDPA SHOWING OFF AMANDA MICHELLE.

ONE OF PERRY'S FIRST TELETHONS ON THE CTN NETWORK IN CLEARWATER, FL.
THIS WOULD OPEN THE DOOR FOR MANNA-FEST TEN YEARS LATER.

ONE OF PERRY'S ILLUSTRATED SERMONS
AT THE DALTON CAMPMEETING

PREPARING THE FIRST TELEVISION SET
IN THE NEW STUDIO IN 1998.

JOE VANKOEVERING, HOST OF GOD'S NEWS BEHIND THE NEWS,
CONDUCTING AN INTERVIEW FOR HIS WEEKLY PROGRAM.

THE MANNA-FEST PRODUCTION TRUCK, USED TO TAPE MAJOR MINISTRY EVENTS
AND UPLINK SATELLITE TRANSMISSION.

GEORGE W. BUSH SIGNED THIS PHOTO IN NOVEMBER OF 2000.
IT WAS TAKEN IN 1998 NEAR THE WESTERN WALL IN ISRAEL.

THE 25,000 SQUARE FOOT MINISTRY CENTER WAS DEDICATED DEBT FREE ON MAY 15, 1998.

SHIPPING THE HUGE SPORTS CARD COLLECTION TO WORLD HARVEST CHURCH IN OHIO.
THIS ACT WAS THE KEY OF OBEDIENCE FOR OUR MINISTRY BUILDING BEING DEBT FREE.

MARCUS AND JONI LAMB AND FAMILY.
PERRY WAS ON THE SET THE FIRST NIGHT
DAYSTAR WAS ON THE AIR!

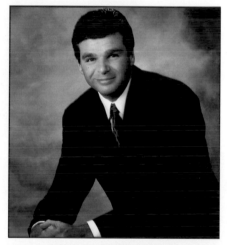

PERRY MET JENTEZEN FRANKLIN
DURING A THREE WEEK REVIVAL IN GASTONIA, NC
RIGHT AFTER PERRY AND PAM WERE MARRIED.

PERRY WENT TO TAMPA, FL AND PREACHED THE FIRST REVIVAL AT RANDY
AND PAULA WHITE'S CHURCH WHEN THEY HAD ONLY 27 MEMBERS!

PERRY'S DEAR FRIEND OF 20 YEARS – GIDEON SHOR,
THE BEST ISRAELI TOUR GUIDE AROUND!

THE KRAFTS—OWNERS OF THE NEW ENGLAND
PATRIOTS, SUPER BOWL WINNERS.

AN IN-DEPTH DISCUSSION WITH PROPHECY SCHOLAR HAL LINDSEY.

PREPARING GROUND FOR OUR
CURRENT MINISTRY OFFICE.

EVANGELIST MILDRED COLLINS. EVERY YOUNG MAN
CONVERTED TO CHRIST UNDER HER MINISTRY WAS
LATER CALLED TO PREACH, INCLUDING FRED STONE.

DRAWINGS FROM 1999 OF THE VISION OF THE FIVE TORNADOES.
WE KNOW THIS WAS THE SEPTEMBER 11TH ATTACKS.

THE BOOK AND MAPS THAT PERRY USED TO SOLVE THE "TREASURE MYSTERY."

THE DAY PAM ANNOUNCED SHE HAD CONCEIVED
A CHILD (JONATHAN), WE WERE OVERJOYED.

PERRY AND JONATHAN AT
SUPER BOWL XXXVIII IN 2004.

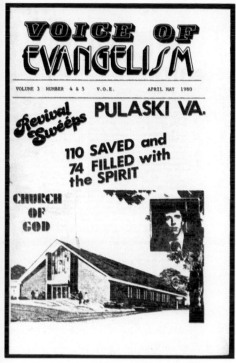

ONE OF THE EARLY VOICE OF EVANGELISM MAGAZINES

AN EARLY MAGAZINE PUBLISHED BY T.L. LOWERY
THAT INSPIRED PERRY TO PUBLISH HIS OWN MAGAZINE

GOD BLESSES OUR REGIONAL MEETINGS WITH GREAT ATTENDANCE AND SPIRITUAL RESULTS.

JOHN AND LUCY BAVA (CENTER) AND FAMILY, CHRISTMAS 1994.

OUR ISRAEL TOURS HAVE BECOME A HIGHLIGHT OF EACH YEAR!

PAM MEETING WITH PARTNERS IN HER OFFICE AT THE DEDICATION OF THE NEW BUILDING IN MAY, 1998.

PERRY AND JONATHAN PREPARING FOR
JONATHAN'S KINDERGARTEN GRADUATION.

BEA OGLE AND HER HUSBAND, ELROY.
"AUNT BEA" FOUNDED THE DAUGHTERS OF RACHEL
AND HAS BEEN A V.O.E. PARTNER FOR MANY YEARS.

PERRY WITH JOYCE AND DAVID MEYER

PERRY WITH JOEL OSTEEN (LEFT) AND ROMAN GABRIEL III

PERRY, PAM, AND AMANDA WITH JUANITA BYNUM

PERRY WITH CHRISTIAN SINGER CARMAN

PERRY WITH DARLENE BISHOP

PERRY, PAM, AND JONATHAN WITH IVAN PARKER (SECOND FROM LEFT).

THE RIBBON CUTTING CEREMONY AT THE DEDICATION OF OUR CURRENT MINISTRY OFFICE IN MAY, 1998.

THE WHITE HOUSE THAT SAT ON THE CURRENT VOE PROPERTY. THE FORMER OWNER USED TO SIT ON THE PORCH AND PRAY ABOUT SPREADING THE GOSPEL!

RECOGNIZING GRANDMA BAVA (IN THE RED JACKET) FOR BEING OUR LONGEST CONTINUING PARTNER.

JOSEPH IS OUR MAIN DRIVER ON THE HOLY LAND TOURS.

OUR MINISTRY TEAM EATING CRAWFISH AT DR. MELILLI'S HOUSE IN BATON ROUGE, LA.

ONE OF MY FIRST REVIVALS IN THE ONLY
SUIT I OWNED AT THE TIME!

ROBERT & CHERYL GESING HAVE GREATLY
ASSISTED OUR MINISTRY OVER THE YEARS.

THE NIGHT IN NOVEMBER 1999 WHEN THE LORD DIRECTED US TO START A TV PROGRAM.

MARCUS LAMB GIVING A PROPHETIC WORD OF KNOWLEDGE AT OUR CAMPMEETING.

JONATHAN AT THE GARDEN TOMB IN ISRAEL

WHO IS THAT MASKED MAN?

PERRY PREACHING AT THE LIGHTHOUSE CHURCH IN KENYA, AFRICA

A REVIVAL AT RANDY WHITE'S TENT, WHICH ONCE CAUGHT FIRE. IT DID NOT BURN DOWN BECAUSE IT WAS FIREPROOF.

AMANDA VISITS HER DAD AT HIS OFFICE DURING THE WORKDAY

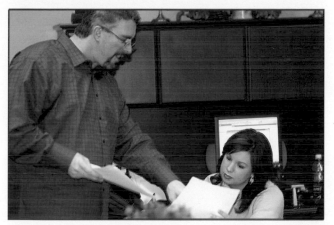

GINA BEAN AND PERRY ANSWER QUESTIONS FROM EMAILS

PAM READING HER PERSONAL MAIL FROM A MINISTRY PARTNER

We love and appreciate our friends and partners so much! Thanks for believing in us.

times when we must work overtime, and traveling can still become hectic. However, I do not book the long, extended meetings anymore. Burning out is not on the agenda.

A few months later, the wonderful and romantic fall months arrived in the Tennessee mountains, I arose from my bed and realized that there was no cloud of darkness, nor spirit of heaviness on me, in me or around me. The very air seemed charged and the atmosphere was clear. Perhaps during the night hours, while I slept, an angel of the Lord had slipped into the house and cut the bands of darkness around my head. He whispered into my spirit, "It's okay; he's free now."

I stepped into the shower singing. I grabbed Pam, gave her a big kiss, and headed to the office on Broad Street in south Cleveland. Stepping into my office, I grabbed my Bible and slapped the desk, yelling at the top of my lungs, "Tell the devil, 'Stone is back!' " Thank God I've been "back" ever since, and I'm not finished yet!

LESSONS I HAVE LEARNED IN THESE EXPERIENCES

♦ Before a major attack, God will give you warnings if you will listen.

♦ Don't forget that the Lord has planned a way out for you before the attack comes.

♦ You are not Superman. If Jesus needed a break from ministry, so do you.

♦ Don't try to fight the enemy by yourself.

♦ Expose the attack to the light, and the enemy has no place to hide.

♦ The trouble you go to bed with tonight may be gone when you get up in the morning.

♦ God can release in a short time the trials you have carried for a long time.

CHAPTER 8

PAM'S WARNING DREAM FROM GOD

For God may speak in one way,

or in another. . . . In a dream, in

a vision of the night, when deep

sleep falls . . . He opens the ear

. . . and seals . . . instruction (Job

33:14-16).

PAM'S WARNING DREAM FROM GOD

(This chapter is from Pam's perspective)

Marriage is an amazing miracle. Two people from different families and backgrounds become one flesh and must learn to give and take, bless and rebuke, laugh and cry, and come through tough times smiling.

At some point, every marriage will hit a bump in the road. Sometimes couples encounter a pothole, and at other times a huge roadblock. Being able to make it past these times and survive, emerging stronger than before, should be the goal of every husband and wife.

Women have a God-given instinct to know when something isn't right, especially if another woman is involved. I have told Perry, "No woman knows another woman like a woman." If the serpent in the garden had been a woman, Adam and Eve would still be in the garden. Eve would have discerned what that old snake was after and would have said, "You old snake! You are trying to get my husband and you can't have him. Get out of that tree and get out of this garden before I throw you out!"

During our many years of marriage, I have always trusted Perry regarding the opposite sex. For over 19 years I traveled with him continually, and we were together like Siamese twins. When I am not traveling with Perry, one or two male co-workers always travel with him and stay with him from the beginning of the journey to the end. This is so no one can make a false claim against him. Perry also has developed several private security guidelines he keeps when traveling, that are only known to his inner circle.

At times people may feel that Perry is somewhat cold and un-friendly or rather quiet, especially if they see or meet him out-side of the pulpit or a church setting. He is not unfriendly. He simply exercises caution and discretion with those he may not know well.

We have over 24 employees in the ministry office. We con-sider the male and female workers dear friends in whom we have confidence and trust. On two occasions, however, I sensed some form of danger on the horizon for my husband.

THE FIRST WOMAN

I felt this first woman was actually having problems in her relationship with her husband. She was a good Christian woman, but seemed to *need* special attention. When I told Perry to be careful because I felt she needed attention she was not getting at home, Perry thought I was being a little "hyper." Men usually pick up on the obvious but not on the little things.

Perry became close to this person. They even worked together to form a small partnership involving a form of ministry. Eventu-ally, things did not jell and the partnership broke apart, and Perry allowed the flame of close friendship to begin to diminish. Many months later, the husband separated from the woman because of his own personal problems. We were both saddened for them and their children. I felt that if Perry had been too close to her during her divorce, however, they may have leaned on one another for moral support, which could have formed a much stronger emotional tie.

MY WARNING DREAMS

I am not a person who experiences many dreams. When I do dream, it will often carry either a spiritual or a literal meaning. Years ago, I dreamed of a pastor's wife who had become pregnant again after she had several children. I saw her sitting alone in a room and saying to herself, "I can't take this anymore." She was so discouraged that I was afraid she might be tempted to actually harm herself.

The next day, on Wednesday, Perry returned from an overseas trip and I met him at the airport. "We must go to church tonight and see this couple," I insisted. That night we showed up unannounced. The pastor was speaking, but his wife was not in church. After service, I asked the woman's mother where she was. She responded, "She is at home tonight. You know she is pregnant again don't you?"

My heart began to pound and I knew I had a warning from the Lord. That night we went to their house and I shared my dream. She and her husband began crying. They were so stressed out that they had talked about giving up the church. That night God lifted their spirits, and today God is prospering their ministry.

After Perry told me about the battle he had experienced, I had a strange dream. I dreamed I was standing at a large metal fence with another woman. Just over the fence was a huge spider, a dead tarantula with a large dagger sticking in its heart. For some reason I felt as though this represented a strong friendship Perry had been in, and which he had suddenly severed, placing a dagger in the heart.

Suddenly, a woman beside me said, "Look coming over the hill." I saw another tarantula the exact same size and color moving over the hill. I knew this spider was headed toward me.

When I told Perry about the dream, he said, "A spider weaves a web. A tarantula lulls its prey to sleep and then kills it." He believed it was a warning about a female that would try to weave a web around him by going through me.

That same night, I told him I had dreamed of a female, a minister's wife, who appeared to be planning to try to seduce Perry in a hotel room. We both believed the second spider could be a warning related to this woman.

Oddly enough, in a few weeks this minister's wife came to one of our meetings in Florida. She and her husband stayed at the same hotel we were staying in. The woman was a singer and was planning to produce a new singing tape. Knowing Perry had experience in songwriting and tape production, she approached him and asked him to write some songs for her. She inquired if he would personally help her with her new tape.

Perry told me about the invitation to help, but said, "I didn't fall off the turnip truck yesterday. I would be a living fool to link myself with this woman, after you had a dream of that spider coming our way." The next day he immediately turned down the offer, to the great dismay of the woman.

It Was an Accurate Warning

Years later we received a call from a pastor's wife. This same couple had been conducting a revival in their church. The minister was a powerful evangelist. His wife (this same young woman) would leave the parsonage at 10 o'clock in the morning and not return until nearly church time. After several weeks they discovered she was spending time with one of the men in the church.

Months later, she left her husband for another man. It was discovered she had been unfaithful to her husband. We were very sad for the couple and for those who loved them. In retrospect, we are both thankful for the warnings given to us in advance, before the enemy gained access into our lives. A warning must be heeded, however.

I believe the Lord can and will protect a person from unseen assignments of the enemy, but we must all be sensitive to obey the warnings we receive. Every marriage will have bumps, road-blocks and detours that will come in the relationship. You must be determined to make the journey despite the obstacles, and work through each obstacle together.

With wisdom you both can make it through the tests of life and come out stronger in your relationship.

Not all attacks will come from the opposite sex. The fiery darts of the enemy are sent against your finances, your children and your health.

Together, we look back over the many years of marriage and see how the Lord has protected us. We have enjoyed many years together, but we are not finished yet!

LESSONS I HAVE LEARNED FROM THIS EXPERIENCE

♦ No one knows a woman like another woman.

♦ Your husband does not always have the discernment you may have.

♦ Discuss openly with each other situations that appear to be a danger.

♦ God will warn you and give you a plan of action to help preserve your marriage.

CHAPTER 9

THE HORSE IS NOT YOUR SOURCE

Some trust in chariots, and some in horses, but we will remember the name of the Lord our God (Psalm 20:7).

THE HORSE IS NOT YOUR SOURCE

At times I am asked, "What is the greatest lesson you have learned in your entire ministry?" Without hesitation I recall the time when the Holy Spirit gave me a powerful word, through a personal incident, telling me, "The horse is not your source." This statement will require a detailed account of the most unique lesson I have ever learned.

A HIDDEN TREASURE WORTH $500,000

In the mid 1980's, Pam and I concluded a revival at the Adamsville, Alabama, Church of God. We traveled to Georgia for a football game between the University of Georgia and the University of Alabama, which is Pam's favorite team. Arriving a few hours prior to the game we stumbled into the University's main bookstore, and began browsing through shelves holding thousands of books. My attention was drawn to a strange book that looked like it belonged more in the children's book section than a university bookstore.

The illustrated cover featured a carousel and a young girl carrying a book, weaving her way through a maze. The title was *Treasure*. In the corner was a photograph of a gold horse. I picked up the book and flipped through the pages. On the outside back cover were the words:

A $500,000

TREASURE

is hidden somewhere in America

It could be yours!

Solve the hidden puzzle and lay claim to the most fabulous contest in history.

All the clues you need are in this book.

The book revealed that a safety deposit box key was hidden in the belly of a golden horse, which was valued at $25,000. Inside the deposit box was a certificate redeemable for $500,000 to the person who could solve the puzzle. The certificate would pay $25,000 a year for 20 years. I began to think about what the ministry could do with $500,000. We could get some needed office space, buy important equipment and help to build foreign churches. I reasoned, "Perhaps this is why I'm at this game and in this bookstore. Could the Lord help me solve this puzzle to have additional money for the ministry?"

My curiosity was stirred, and I purchased the book. At the opening kickoff, Pam was standing on her feet and I was sitting down with the book, making notes. Throughout the game, she would punch me in the side and say, "What in the world has your attention?" The game concluded and we checked into a local hotel for the night. As Pam rested in bed, I sat up with the book and a notepad, and with the desk lamp glowing in the darkness until 5 o'clock in the morning. In just seven hours, I had solved part of the puzzle. I knew which state the treasure was buried in and even the area of the state where the golden horse was hidden.

I solved this by taking the first letter of the first word in each of the 21 chapters to see if it would spell anything. Here is an actual list of the letters:

The Chapter	*The first letter in the chapter*
Chapter 1	T
Chapter 2	I
Chapter 3	G
Chapter 4	N
Chapter 5	O
Chapter 6	R
Chapter 7	E
Chapter 8	S
Chapter 9	T
Chapter 10	A
Chapter 11	T
Chapter 12	E
Chapter 13	S
Chapter 14	H
Chapter 15	A
Chapter 16	P
Chapter 17	E
Chapter 18	S
Chapter 19	A
Chapter 20	T
Chapter 21	A

The first four letters spell absolutely nothing. From chapter 5 through chapter 21, however, the letters begin forming the statement:

ORE STATE SHAPES AT A

The only state with the name abbreviated *ORE* is the northwestern state of Oregon. I questioned, "What does the rest of the phrase mean, *SHAPES AT A*?" Throughout the book there were drawings of various things. In each chapter with the first word beginning in the letter A, the shape of the drawing was in the form of the state of Oregon.

The second clue was a picture of a round globe with a series of small maps cut out in the center of the globe. In the center of the globe was a map of Crater Lake State Park, which happens to be located in the state of Oregon. I began to study the book from the premise that the golden horse was buried at Crater Lake State Park in Orgeon.

After returning home, I continued to break small codes throughout the book. I noticed that on several pages of the book there were small sections of a map. When pieced together, they form one large map. I went to a copy machine and copied the pieces of the map, pasting them together with clear tape. The map formed a square with a circle in the middle. There were numerous arrows pointing from within the circle. There were four horses spaced in four locations on the outside square. This again pointed to Crater Lake State Park.

The park itself is built around a circular lake of water. It was once a volcano. In the lake itself is a small island, called Wizard Island. There are four viewing points around the lake, which are identified on the map with the four horses. The X on the map is the site of the island.

The more clues that were broken, the more I was convinced that the horse was buried on the island located in the midst of the lake.

One of the clues said to begin searching during the spring. Because of snow, the park is not opened until springtime. The title of chapter 13 was "The Lodge." I learned that there was a lodge in the park. After sharing the information with Pam, I contacted a personal friend, Keith Dudley, to join me in a journey to the state of Oregon on the West Coast. Keith thought I was a few bricks short of a load, but as a friend he was ready to enjoy the journey and the scenery.

We flew to Portland and rented a car for the journey to Crater Lake. Arriving at our destination, I was overwhelmed by the astonishing natural beauty of God's creation. We stood overlooking the lake, and I began to scope out the top rim of the island for any clues that may give me the exact location of the buried treasure. We checked into the hotel—an old lodge, complete with rugged, but comfortable, rooms and a nice restaurant.

When we walked out of our room into the hallway toward the restaurant, I was stunned to see a mounted deer's head in the hallway. On page 53 of the book, in the section called "The Lodge," there was a drawing similar to what we were staring at! I told Keith, "Look at this! There is no doubt we are at the right spot."

The next morning we headed toward the boat dock to take a small boat to the island. Arriving at the base of the old volcanic island, we then headed up a walking trail to the rim on top. I remember the excitement building as we climbed higher. At the top there was nothing to see but old black rocks, dead trees, some shrubs and a few tall pines. We took a right turn and ended up sitting on a large pile of stones.

I began to review the book and the pages of notes I had made. Something was missing, and I could not pinpoint the main clue. The entire afternoon was spent on one side of the island's rim. Late that evening I stepped about 10 feet into the old volcano and found a rock pointing to the other side, with the date 1886 carved on it. This was a major clue. We returned to take the boat back to the lodge. I took the book out and found the missing link. There was a fellow with a black umbrella, and on the umbrella were lines and geometic designs. I realized I was on the wrong side of the rim.

The Tree Shaped like a Horseshoe

The next morning I hung a 30-pound backpack over my shoulders, and Keith and I headed back to the boat dock. As the boat passed the other side of the island, I caught a glimpse of a large, bent-over tree, bleached white. Using your imagination, it could be a small gate. This was the section of the path I should have taken, turning left at the top of the rim and not right.

Walking briskly, we soon reached the top of the rim. I went past the white tree and saw a strange site. Hidden behind a large pine tree was an old tree perfectly shaped like a horseshoe. I began to notice that the rocks took on certain forms similar to the shapes I had found in the book. I followed a path that curved into the rim and exited out the opposite side. There, I was stunned to see a tree lying on the ground, in the form of a large horseshoe.

At the end of the tree, the old dried root looked exactly like a horse's head on a carousel! This is why the carousel is prominent on the cover of the book. As I moved some small vines covering the U shape of the tree, I saw three solid granite stones lying in the U. They were hidden under the vines and were about eight inches deep.

By this time Keith Dudley was a believer! He was saying, "This is unreal. I can't believe it! This tree is shaped like a horseshoe and the root looks the head of a horse." I reminded him, "That's not the only odd part. Look at these three stones. These are not volcanic rocks, they are granite. They have been placed here as a clue! The horse is buried right here."

By now I was whispering, fearful someone may come up behind us. Every clue fit. Every detail was there. I reached into my backpack and pulled out the video camera. Keith started taping and I took a small trowel and begin picking at the dirt. I was unprepared for the ground to be this hard. I noticed that some of the vines were old and dried up and had been cut, as though someone had previously dug in the exact area.

As the hole became deeper—I actually dug down about 12 inches—I remembered that the only clue I had not solved was how deep the horse was buried. One of the clues said not to dig too deep. But what was too deep? As time passed, Keith commented, "I wouldn't go too much deeper." Since the day was wearing away and only one more boat would pick up the last visitors to the island, we both assumed someone had already located the spot and dug up the horse.

The fact that the dirt was still in place, however, and that the three granite stones were lying in the horseshoe shaped tree made me think, *Could it be here at a deeper level?* I had already dug about 18 inches in the ground and to no avail.

Had I returned to the book, I would have noticed a drawing of a rag doll with black shoes. The doll had two feet, which indicated I was to dig two feet deep! I actually stopped six inches short.

THE REAL TREASURE

Returning to Portland the next day, I was confused. I knew, without a doubt, that I had solved the puzzle in minute detail, up to the very spot where the gold horse was buried. I was meditating on why the Lord allowed me to make the journey and return empty-handed. Keith was driving and we were listening to a Christian radio station. Suddenly, the announcer introduced a song I had never heard before and have not heard since. It was called "Treasure," which ironically was the same name of the book!

The singer began telling of a man who took a journey to look for a treasure and came back empty. At the end of the journey the man in the song discovered that the Lord was his greatest treasure. Keith and I kept looking at each other. I actually heard the Holy Spirit speaking deep within me, "I allowed you to solve this because it was something you wanted to do and something you enjoyed. I did not let you find it, however, because *the horse is not your source!*"

I suddenly began crying and rejoicing at the same time. Keith looked at me and I began yelling, "The horse is not my source! God is going to give me what I need when I need it to accomplish what I need to accomplish. I don't need a golden horse when I have a Great God!"

WHAT HAPPENED TO THE GOLDEN HORSE?

The golden horse remained in that exact spot for several months. While preaching in Pulaski, Virginia, the local paper told the story of the golden horse and how no one claimed the prize; so it was turned over to Big Brothers of America. Those who removed the horse used a pick and shovel to remove the dirt.

For several months I had a videotape of the entire trip, including the tree shaped like a horseshoe and evidence of me removing the three granite rocks and digging into the soil in search of the treasure. We have never figured out what happed to the video, but we have not been able to find it for some time. Pam and I think we left it at a pastor's home (we would show it to close friends).

Some people today are seeking a golden horse of a different kind. They ask the Lord to give them the numbers to the giant Powerball lottery, pledging that if they strike it big the Lord will be guaranteed His share of the take. As the jackpot rises, some people will spend their entire paycheck, and even take their nest egg from bank accounts, to purchase numerous tickets—with the gut feeling they will hit it big.

When they fail to produce, they are left with less money, disappointed, and waiting for the next pot of gold at the end of the rainbow. God's way of blessing His people is established through the obedience of tithing and giving.

The Almighty has promised to bless the works of our hands and prosper our mind and spirit with creative ideas and witty inventions. I am no longer digging for gold, but I'm preaching for souls, and I am not finished preaching yet!

What I Have Learned in these Experiences

- ♦ There is no limit to what a Spirit-filled believer can do— including solving mysteries.

- ♦ We must not rely on the things of the world to be our provision and our source.

- ♦ If God gives you the plans, He will give you the provision to accomplish those plans.

- ♦ Some trust in chariots and some in horses—but I will trust in the Lord.

- ♦ God can release the money you need when you need it.

CHAPTER 10

THE AMAZING BIRTH OF MANNA-FEST

[He] rained down manna on them to eat . . . bread of heaven. Men ate angels' food; He sent them food to the full (Psalm 78:24, 25).

THE AMAZING BIRTH OF MANNA-FEST

In February 1988, we conducted a revival at the Church of God in Zephyrhills, Florida, where Tom Jammes was pastor. At 6 o'clock in the evening, Tom knocked on our bedroom door and said, "Perry you need to see this." I went into the living room where a news commentator was showing a brief clip of evangelist Jimmy Swaggart coming off his airplane in Louisiana. The newsman was reporting that Jimmy had been called to the Assembly of God headquarters in Springfield, Missouri, on charges of illicit behavior with a female.

At the time, we all suspected it was another attempt by the media to boost their sagging ratings with a new and sensational rumor. However, the commentator had details that were troubling. I went to the telephone immediately to call a member of my board of directors, whose father-in-law and mother-in-law served on Swaggart's ministry board. Rick Towe answered the phone from his home in Chattanooga, Tennessee.

"Rick, they are reporting down in Florida that something has happened with Swaggart." I said. "Is there anything to this?"

Rick paused for several seconds and said, "Clyde just got off the phone with Jimmy. He called him and said there was a story that was going to break in the media."

"Rick, is it true?" I inquired, hoping he would say, "No, it is not." "Yes," he said in a low tone. "I'm afraid there is something to it."

"Is a woman really involved in this?"

"I'm not sure of the details," Rick replied. "It involves some form of pornography with a woman." I hung up the phone and told Pam, "It's true." We were both saddened and in shock. Swaggart had the largest Pentecostal ministry in the world and had the ear of entire nations overseas. In South America, people in the bars would turn the channel to hear the man preach.

My heart felt like it was going to drop to the floor. I could not believe it! This man had the largest ministry in the world, and I wondered, *What will happen now?* The body of Christ had gone through a severe trial with the PTL scandal, and Swaggart had been an outspoken critic of Bakker. On national television he had called Jim a "cancer in the body of Christ." Now, as old-timers would say, "The chickens had come home to roost." The weakness Swaggart had criticized in Bakker's life was now at Swaggart's own doorstep.

Time would reveal that Swaggart's root sin was pride, and the sin with the women was the fruit and not the root. That night the entire church was heavy-hearted. The pastor and I were so concerned about the incident and its impact on the body of Christ that, after the service, we chose to return to the church around midnight and spend the night in prayer.

THE WORD OF THE LORD CAME TO ME

As we travailed under a great prayer burden, the minutes turned into hours. By 3 o'clock in the morning, I was lying on my back on the front pew in the sanctuary. Everything was now peaceful and quiet. The presence of God had filled the small church. Suddenly, I heard a clear voice say MANNA-FEST.

I immediately sat up and realized it was not "manifest", but two words—*manna* and *fest*—alluding to manna, the food Israel ate in the wilderness; and fest, which is the abbreviation for "festival." I thought, *Where did that come from?* Then I heard this clear statement in my spirit, "This will be the title of your television program."

Now I was sitting up and laughing inside. Not only was I not interested in a television program, I had no money for a program. I didn't even own a video camera or a video recorder. I had no office space for a television studio. I knew I had heard from the Lord, however. We returned to the pastor's house and after several hours of sleep, I told Pam about the incident. I told her not to tell anyone about it, and to keep the name **Manna-Fest** secret, because someone could try to take this name from us. We both hid this revelation in our spirits until the time came, many years later, to share it openly.

The crisis with Swaggart exploded in the body of Christ like a nuclear bomb. We continued to travel and minister in extended revivals. Instead of a decline in attendance and support, the impact of the meetings increased and the finances continued to come in for ministry. It seemed people wanted to support someone they could see, hear and touch personally—someone who had credibility with the local church and the local pastor.

THE VISION IN LEEDS, ALABAMA

In July, six months after the visitation in Florida, we were ministering in Leeds, Alabama. Pastor Victor Massey's church was too small for the crowds, so a tent was erected to accommo-date the attendance. The heat was almost unbearable, and the temperature was often 100 degrees in the shade an hour before the service! Yet, the people poured onto the church grounds and filled the tent.

During the third week of this revival, I experienced a confir-mation of the word the Lord had given me in Florida. In the early hours of the morning, I experienced an unusual night vision. A night vision is similar to a dream, but in a night vision you are fully aware of where you are and what you are experiencing. All five senses operate and the vision is three dimensional and in full color. The only difference between this form of a vision and a normal vision is that a night vision happens when you are asleep, and a normal vision can happen while you are awake or in prayer.

In this vision I was walking up a grass-covered hill. In front of me was a paved road and in front of the road was a set of concrete steps. At the end of the steps some type of tower appeared, with several small dishes attached to it. I knew it was not a shortwave tower or a radio tower. Years later I would see one at the TBN (Trinity Boradcasting Network) station in Atlanta, Georgia. A simi-lar tower sits behind the TBN building and is a microwave tower that transmits the signal from the station to the satellite.

The tower in my vision was situated at the top of a small hill, at the end of the concrete steps. To the right of the large tower stood a man with white hair, dressed in a black suit, a white shirt and a tie. He appeared to be about 6' 4" and had a clear olive complexion. He addressed me as "son" and proceeded to give me this message: "Son, if you will do the following, this is what the Lord will give to you."

First, he told me something that was so personal that I have not felt a release to share it with anyone, except a few close friends. He then said, "You must preach where God tells you to preach. You must preach the message God tells you to preach. If you do these things, God will give you this!"

When I awoke from this vision, I felt it involved some form of a television ministry. What did the man mean when he said, "God is going to give you this?" Was it a television program, a studio to tape a program, or a television station? Was he predicting I would one day have a station, or a network?

The next morning I shared this vision with my lovely wife. The full meaning would not be known until years later, when we were purchasing property for our new ministry center. Between the time of the vision and the full understanding, another strange confirmation came in a rather unusual way.

IT WAS A BOY AND NOT A GIRL

Most of my early partners remember me telling them at the Pigeon Forge Campmeeting in the fall of 1988, that I had a dream of seeing a little girl with bangs and a "prissy personality." She told me her name was Amanda, and she was my little girl! At the time we had no children, but in 1989 Pam became pregnant.

We were in Leeds, Alabama, again, ministering in a large ware-house, when Pam and her friend, Tracy Davis, drove to Cleveland for Pam's sonogram. Pam returned before the service ended with a small picture, and announced, "It appears to be a boy!" I said, "How can this be when I saw this little girl?" She said, "Maybe the girl will come later!"

By faith I painted the room pink, and some friends gave us girl clothes instead of boy clothes. On December 23, Pam's water broke and I drove her to the Bradley Memorial Hospital on the coldest day in the history of Cleveland. The wind chill was below zero.

After five hours of labor, at 5:50 in the morning, I saw a little "cone-head" infant come forth from the birth canal. I screamed, "It's a boy!" The doctor said, "Were you expecting something different?" I didn't take the time to explain. We had a child and we were happy. The problem was we never chose a boy's name!

"What will you name him?" the nurse asked.

"We don't know yet." Pam replied, still catching her breath.

"Can I let you know a little later on?" I asked the doctor.

"Sure, but don't wait too long, we need to make out the birth certificate." We decided on the name *Jonathan*, but I wanted the right middle name.

After spending some "bonding time" with Mom and the child, I said, "Honey I want to get a few hours sleep. All this labor has worn ME out!" Returning home to a quiet house, I lay down and prayed, "Lord, give me the name YOU want this boy to have. You said in your Word that the male child who opens up the womb is holy (Luke 2:23). He is your baby, Lord!"

I closed my eyes to doze off, and in a moment's time I saw a clear picture flash before me. It was a beautiful design-like drawing. I saw an angel with his head pointed upward and a large silver trumpet to his mouth. He was standing with one foot flat on the ground, and the other foot behind him at an angle, with his toes touching the ground. Large, red words appeared in the form of Roman style letters:

Gabriel Communications Network

I sat up on the living room couch and thought, *There it is again, something connected to communications and spreading the gospel.* I knew the angel Gabriel announced the birth of the Messiah when He came the first time. It appeared the Lord was revealing to me that some form of global communications would be connected to my ministry.

Suddenly I yelled out, "Gabriel! I'll call his middle name Gabriel. He was born two days before Christmas, and Gabriel was the angel announcing Christ's birth. Jonathan Gabriel Stone, that's a good name!" Thus, my firstborn son received his full name.

Knowing that God had given me the name *Gabriel Communications Network*, I immediately began the legal process of securing the name legally. I wanted the name to be on legal record so no one else could claim it. I did the same with Manna-Fest.

Both names were cleared, and we own the full rights to both of them. A few months after we filed, the Catholics were starting a television network and chose the name Gabriel Communications Network. Our office received a call and was asked if we would be willing to give up that name or sell it. I refused, reminding my office manager that this was the name the Lord gave me. Today the official legal papers hang on the wall outside our television studio and the prophecy videos are often placed under the name of Gabriel Communications Network.

The lawyers for a world renowned ministry called and asked if they could use the name Manna-fest for five years as the name for their main ministry event. They even offered to purchase the legal right from us. I refused and told my lawyer that these names were birthed in prayer by the Holy Spirit and were my spiritual inheritance. I was not going to be like Esau and sell my spiritual birthright and blessing that the Lord had assigned to me.

THE CALL FROM CTN IN FLORIDA

A year later, during our second visit to Zephyrhills, Florida, (where the Lord had given me the name Manna-fest), something happened that would set the course for our entire ministry. As my friend, Dr. E.L. Terry, always said, "There will be a moment in your life when God gets in your shoes and will thrust you into your destiny." That moment came.

Pastor Tom Jammes had set me up to be interviewed on the air by CTN (Christian Television Network), a well known Christian television station in Clearwater, Florida. They would interview me on the subject of Bible prophecy. At the time, CTN had a daily flagship program called, "The Good Life." It was interview-oriented and hosted by the founder, Bob DeAndrea, and at times by a wonderful woman of God, Arthlene Rippy.

Without really knowing me, Arthlene took the pastor's recommendation and invited me to appear "live" as a guest. This was my first real television appearance, yet I was very comfortable with the concept. That day I dealt with recent events in prophecy, and when they opened up the phone lines for questions, the lines jammed. The response was great. Even Arthlene was pleasantly surprised. "You need to come back some time and do this again," she suggested. "I would love to," I responded.

After the program Tom Jammes said, "Perry, this is part of God's call on your life. I believe He is going to open doors for you in the media of television."

One Idea from the Holy Spirit

You will discover that everything begins with an idea. "God ideas" are always creative, and lead to success in whatever field you are. In the early 1990s, the Lord had given me a "God idea."

I had been to Israel several times, and carried a photographer to document the places of interest, especially in Biblical prophecy. For several years I would announce a special prophecy update for Saturday night, using slides from Israel. Prophecy night always drew the largest attendance during every revival. People packed the churches, literally from wall to wall, to see and hear the messages. They were also the best opportunity we had to win souls to Christ, which is always my ultimate goal.

Eventually, people were asking if I had this material on a video tape. I knew a church in Lenoir City that had a television studio with television equipment. After prayer, the Holy Spirit impressed me to produce videos using the slides. I would sit in a chair and teach. A small remote was in my left hand that was attached to the slide projector in another room. A still camera was placed in the dark room and I would change the slides from where I was sitting!

It was not the best way of taping, but it was the only available means I had. One day I actually taught for 10 hours straight, using slides and visual aids. The videos became, and are still today, the most popular teaching tools we have.

CTN CALLS BACK

"Perry, this is CTN in Clearwater. Bob DeAndrea wanted me to call and ask if you have any of your prophecy material on tape, especially on video tape?"

"I have just completed a new prophecy series on video," I responded.

"Would it be possible for you to teach at our upcoming telethon? We could offer your video tapes as a premium to those who support the station with their giving."

I had seen telethons a few times on TBN, but had never participated in one. I liked the idea of teaching, but I wasn't sure about a "telethon." My reputation among close ministry friends was that I was the world's worst at receiving an offering.

My mind went back to my first Pigeon Forge camp meeting in November, 1988. The three-night, five-service event drew about 600 people to the convention center. At the conclusion of the meeting, I was $3,000 in debt. I didn't have the money to pay the bills and I was depressed, to say the least. I said, "If I can't pay the bills I'll never have another camp meeting. This is my last."

My dear friend, Rick Towe, was the president of an oil company, and he saw my distress. He gave me a check to pay the bills with this challenge, "Perry, if you are going to have bigger meetings, learn to receive an offering or get someone who is anointed to receive it!" I accepted the offer to go to CTN and put together a package of videos.

Secretly, I was fearful of failure. *What if no one calls and I fall flat on my face? They will never ask me back.* Fear of rejection is something I have fought from the time I was a child in grade school. I was nervous about the possibility of failure. Finally, after prayer I said, "Lord, I am going to teach the Word and you take care of the fundraising part." That night I preached on prophecy, and the telethon went so well that it became one of the best nights they had experienced in some time. I have never heard so many telephones ringing at one time. It seemed everyone was interested in the prophecy videos and desired to support Christian television in the process. At that time there were only four men preaching prophecy on television, and the interest was amazing.

A CALL FROM CHANNEL 55

Soon, I received a call from Super Channel 55 in Orlando, Florida. The owner, Claude Bowers, had built a marvelous Christian station in central Florida that was reaching into over four million homes. I was asked to minister on prophecy and offer the same videos. Once again, I was stunned at the response of the people. It seemed the phones rang for hours. I would return to the room and weep, because I realized God's hand was on my efforts.

My mind went back to the small monthly flyer I called the *Voice of Evangelism*. In each issue I would place a Prophecy Update, and research the latest information for my "massive reading audience" of over 5,000 people. Once I became tired, and said to myself, "Why am I wasting all my energy and time doing this research? Most of these people don't care; they probably throw this thing away, anyway!"

That night at the Holiday Inn in Orlando, I realized why the Lord placed the prophetic message in my heart. It was not just for a few thousand readers of a magazine, but for millions of viewers on television. I learned that many seeds we plant are not for the time we plant them, but for a future harvest that may come years from now! When I returned to my office in Cleveland, I went to the research library and found many of the old 8-to-12-page magazines with the Prophecy Updates in them. Much of that printed information is just as important now as it was when I wrote it.

Soon, new inspiration came to produce new videos. But I realized I needed my own studio and our own equipment. In the office on Mimosa Drive, we had a room just large enough for a sit-down studio. Dorothy and Russell Spaulding, two dear and talented friends, came to Cleveland and built our first studio. The finances that came in from the stations offering the prophecy videos was used to purchase several cameras, recorders and lights for our new studio.

For seven years we produced and edited special two-hour teaching videos that were offered to our friends and partners in revivals and were made available through the telethons on Christian stations. Yet, I never felt impressed or directed to have a weekly television program.

Once again the thought of purchasing hundreds of thousands of dollars in air time scared me. Since our ministry does not send out monthly fundraising letters, and we did not at the time have a partner base, I told the Lord, "Personally I am not interested in a television program. If you want me to have one you will have to work out the details."

I continued to tape special videos for 10 years, appearing on Christian networks as a guest and traveling the nation preaching. I still remembered the words in February 1988, at the late-night prayer meeting, "Manna-Fest . . . it will be the title of your television program."

As the ministry grew and we expanded to the new building. A new studio was built and new serial-digital equipment, the best available at the time, was purchased. One day Charlie Ellis, my office manager, came to me and said, "We should be doing more than just videos. God gave us this studio and equipment for a greater purpose." I remembered the vision at Leeds of the man beside the tower. I was just waiting to receive peace in my spirit that it was God's timing to move.

A PROPHETIC WORD

I am not a person who is very high on personal prophecy. I have seen good people's lives and futures ruined by too many so-called prophets who have more "words from the Lord" than the prophets who wrote the Bible. When a prophetic word bears witness with your spirit and your heart, however, it can be received.

In November 1999, we hosted our annual Main Event Camp Meeting at the Grand Hotel in Pigeon Forge, Tennessee. The Saturday night service turned out to be the greatest service of the entire week. That night, Don Channell was directing the praise and worship, along with Thomas Sloan. Thomas and his wife had worked with Jimmy Swaggart ministries for many years as singers and as directors of the band.

As I looked around the platform I realized that six of the singers and musicians had once worked with Swaggart. As strange as it seems, that night my mind went back to 1988 when the news report came of Swaggart's moral failure. These precious people had endured the trials and were powerful ministers in their own right.

Suddenly, Thomas stopped and said, "I have to obey God." There on the platform he began to speak a prophetic word, and the Holy Spirit impressed him that it was time for me to initiate a television program to reach more people with the messages the Lord had given me. That night the entire service took an abrupt turn, as the prophetic Word of the Lord began to pour forth like water from a broken dam.

I KNEW THE TIME HAD COME

I asked the Lord, "What is so important about me having a program? Anyone can do this. There are so many ministers on television, I'll just be another voice." The Lord impressed me: "You are going to do things differently. Your message will be different. You will teach the people more than the prophetic Word. You will use unique sets to attract their attention."

We returned from camp meeting and began building some unusual sets. Television is a visual media, and 95 percent of the Christian ministries never use visual props or illustrated messages to reach the masses. I knew we would use more sets, edit more footage, and do things different from the norm. We traveled to Israel to tape programs on location.

We began to contact stations, including Daystar Network, founded by my dear friends, Marcus and Joni Lamb. When I received a contract from Daystar for Monday nights at 7 o'clock EST, I was overwhelmed. I recalled how Marcus and I were two teenage evangelists crisscrossing America in the late 70s and early 80s, having some of the greatest extended revivals in the history of the Church of God.

I recalled his telephone call telling me not to marry the girl I was engaged to. I remember the times we went to the General Assembly and roomed together, staying up half the night talking about the Word of God. I recalled being with Marcus and Joni in Dallas on the opening night of the Daystar Network. I was on the set when Marcus announced, "Ladies and Gentlemen, the Daystar Christian Network is now on the air!"

I knew we had both come a long way . . . and we still had a long way to go! But here was a contract from my friend to his friend. We had been two teenage preachers whose paths had crossed for a future purpose.

As I signed the contract and mailed it with a check, I knew Manna-Fest was not born by the mind of Perry Stone, but in the mind of God. I knew God intended it to be an end-time voice of both prophetic insight and Hebraic teaching of Christian concepts to the body of Christ.

Manna-Fest was launched in September 2000, on CTN, Daystar, Victory Network, and a host of other networks. As a young teenager preaching in Gorman, Maryland, my Grandfather's grandest hope for me was to pastor a church with 100 members and perhaps be a state overseer in the denomination. If you had told me that each year I would owe $1.5 million in air time and have 24 staff members working in a large ministry building, I would have laughed you out of the room.

God's grace has led me and sustained me! Today, I am perhaps halfway through my race. I do not know what hindrances, trials or roadblocks may lie before me on the remaining half of the journey. Grace has brought me safe thus far, however, and grace will lead me on. I just know that we're not finished yet!

Lessons I Have Learned Through this Experience

♦ God may reveal your future in advance, but it may be years before it comes to pass.

♦ Don't jump ahead of God's timing or lag behind.

♦ Don't force God's will, but allow God to open the doors at the proper time.

♦ God will make a plan of provision to help fulfill your vision.

CHAPTER 11

MEETING THE
NEXT UNITED
STATES PRESIDENT

Do you see a man who excels in his work? He will stand before kings; he will stand before unknown men (Proverbs 22:29).

MEETING THE NEXT UNITED STATES PRESIDENT

This event will always stand out as one of the most remarkable of my life to this point. It has been shared many times over the years, and still sparks interest in those who hear it retold. It is one of those events that plays like a movie, with each act building to a climax. It involves a prediction about one of America's presidents.

In April 1998, I was in what I call the "twilight zone." That is the point between being asleep and slightly awake. I heard a clear voice saying, "It is My will for the governor of Texas to be the next president." This was followed by the name of a person who should be his running mate.

I sat up in the bed and awoke my wife—who can sleep through a storm. "Pam, I just heard a voice telling me, 'It is My divine will for the governor of Texas to be the president.' Who is the governor of Texas?" I thought it was the son of former President Bush, but wasn't certain. Pam rolled over, half-awake, and said, "I think he is a Bush." She rolled over and went back to sleep. At that hour she didn't care if Bugs Bunny was running for president!

I immediately arose, shaved and showered, and headed to the office. When Charlie Ellis arrived, he searched on the Internet and confirmed that George W. Bush was indeed the governor. I told Charlie, along with my mother and several others, the word I heard and that I believed it was a revelation from the Holy Spirit. I pondered why this word would come to me at this time, when the election was over 30 months away.

Seven months later, during the week of Thanksgiving, I hosted our annual tour to Israel. The group was scheduled for a desert tour. In my spirit, however, I felt we should remain in Jerusalem and videotape on the Temple Mount. This would prove to be a major decision. The next day was November 29, 1998. The group toured the Temple Mount where we had received permission to videotape inside the Dome of the Rock. After taping, the crew was hanging out near the large green doors that enter the Islamic compound.

Suddenly, my office manger, who was serving as a cameraman, ran up to me and said, "You won't believe who is at the Western Wall." I asked calmly, "Who?" "It is Bush," he blurted out, almost interrupting my one-word question. "Which Bush?" I asked, thinking it might be former President George Bush, or Bush 41, as he is called. "The Bush you said was God's will for him to be president. Right now he is with a group of men headed toward the Western Wall!"

I thought he was playing a joke on me, until I stood on the concrete ramp and saw George W. Bush, Governor of Texas, headed toward the Western Wall. I turned to Charlie and said, "Quick, turn the camera on. I want this on tape." As the tape rolled, I said, "George W. Bush is at the Western Wall in Israel. You might be looking at the next President of the United States." After recording this statement, I said to Charlie, "Quick, let's get down to the wall and see if we can talk to him." By the time we arrived, many from our tour group had already greeted him, and some had suggested he should run for the presidency. A few folks told me later that the governor told them he was uncertain what he would do because he had just been elected for a second term as governor of Texas.

By the time I arrived, Governor Bush was exiting the Western Wall. I went over and greeted him. It was a brief conversation. He asked me where I was from and if I was the fellow who brought the large group. I simply said, "Yes, and they want you to run for president." He nodded in the affirmative, and said, "Okay." A few moments later, a large crowd gathered around him and continued to tell him he was the governor to run for president.

I doubt my encounter or his meeting the tour group had any bearing on his decision, other than some encouragement. I do believe, in retrospect, it happened for my benefit, especially considering the events that followed. I knew without a doubt I had met the next President of the United States. He was in Israel unannounced, and when CNN Jerusalem heard that we had a videotape of Bush at the Western Wall, they offered to buy the tape. We said no.

Word soon spread though the tour group that the Lord had given me a word concerning Bush. The people became rather restless wanting to know, so I shared with the main bus what had happened seven months prior, when the Lord had spoken to me. I never felt impressed to give the name of the other person who "should be his running mate," although I privately told three people so they could confirm it later, if need be.

THE ANNOUNCEMENT CAME

I was not surprised when the governor announced he would run for president. His main opposition was Senator John McCain, who had a great following among independent voters. For a time it appeared that McCain would pass Bush by, until McCain made a serious mistake in the Virginia primary. He verbally attacked the "religious right," and named Jerry Falwell and Pat Robertson. McCain was unaware that both of these ministers had a large constituency in Virginia. The statements backfired on McCain and Bush won Virginia and won his party nomination.

Bush and Gore ran in the 2000 election. In September, Gore led Bush by 18 points. A woman from Kentucky called and said, "I guess Perry is eating his words now." I reminded the person I never said "Bush would be president," only that it was the "will of God." When people get involved, God's will is often not done!

Another Word from the Lord

Six days before the November presidential election, I received a call from Israel Aerobauch, a Jewish believer who ministers with his wife and lives part-time in the country of Israel. He was in town, and asked to come by the office. We shared together for quite some time, and Israel revealed various prophetic events happening in the nation. As always, we concluded our meeting in prayer. This time, the prayer turned prophetic.

As I prayed, the Holy Spirit began to pray through me in one of the languages of the Middle East. Israel understood what the Spirit was saying! He began to yell out, "They are going to try to switch the blessing." He was referring to the story of Jacob crossing his hands, and the child Joseph thought was the son of blessing was not the one God had chosen (Genesis 48:14).

After prayer I asked Israel if he felt the incident involved the upcoming election. He said it was very possible. Suddenly the inspiration of the Holy Spirit came over me and I grabbed a piece of paper, sat at my desk and begin writing these words, "The election of 2000 will be the will of God verses the will of the people." At that moment I had no clue how prophetic this statement was.

THE SPECIAL MEETING IN FLORIDA

The next day I caught a flight to Tampa, Florida, where I was the keynote speaker for the *God's News Behind the News* prophecy banquet. More than 400 people from the surrounding areas of Florida attended this banquet. I knew the Lord would have me the deliver the word, "The Will of God Versus the Will of the People."

My opening statement was, "The election of 2000 will be the will of God versus the will of the people." After hearing the message, Dr. Joe Van Koevering stated the Holy Spirit had told him the State of Florida would determine who the next president would be. Little did anyone know the controversy that would happen four days later.

THE DAY OF THE ELECTION

On Election Day our family was glued to the television reports throughout the evening and throughout the night and the early morning! When the news commentators called Florida for Al Gore, I said to Pam, "It looks like the will of the people prevailed." A few moments later the spokesman for Bush was blasting the media, saying, "Why have you called the state when the polling places are still open on the western side of the state, where Bush's best support is coming from?"

Later estimates said that about 10,000 votes were lost for Bush when people simply left the polling places and did not vote, thinking the election was won. At 3 o'clock in the morning I went to bed.

I got up a few hours later and heard a spokesman for Al Gore say, "The will of the people must be done!" Cold chills ran up my spine. There on the television was a declaration of the battle of the will of God vs. the will of the people. I recalled the prayer meeting when Israel translated the words I was praying, "They will try to reverse the blessing." It appeared Bush had won, but the other side was determined to reverse the decision.

Research in Israel

The controversy about the election continued for weeks. Once again our ministry hosted a tour to Israel. On November 29th, Israel Aerobauch called from the hotel lobby and asked if he could see me. In my hotel room I asked him if he remembered the prayer meeting weeks prior at my office, and he did. Being Jewish, Israel was familiar with how the letters of the Hebrew alphabet are interchanged for numbers. Israel exchanged the English letters of the names Bush and Gore to Hebrew letters and then transliterated the meanings of the letters.

The letters in Bush's name were *bet* (B), *vav* (U) and *shin* (SH). The symbol for *bet* is a house, the *vav* is a hook or connector and the letter *shin* is the 21st letter of the alphabet and the single letter represents the name of God. Israel said, "Bush will be the house connected to God."

We then realized the first Florida recounted vote difference was 300, and the numerical value of the letter *shin*, the last letter in Bush's name, is 300. I realize few, if any, Gentiles would use this system or consider it valid. However, some rabbis would consider these clues to the outcome of the election.

That night our tour group returned to America, departing at 2 o'clock in the morning from Tel Aviv. We were in the ballroom of the hotel for the final dinner when a phone call came for me from Florida. It was Claude Bowers at Channel 55 in Orlando. Claude said that people throughout Florida were asking him to bring me on the station "live," to give any word I believed the Lord had given me. I told him I would fly to Florida on Saturday.

Florida Again

That afternoon I showed for the first time on television, the clip of my meeting President Bush in Israel in 1998. I began to tell the story of how the Lord had spoken to me in 1998 and gave me the word on the "will of God versus the will of the people." In the final part of the program I showed the meaning of Bush's name and the Florida recount numbers linked to the letter *shin*. I said, based on what I was seeing, that Bush would be the 43rd President of the United States. At that moment, Claude opened the phones and they rang literally nonstop. Several Floridians were upset with my "prediction." Some said they would reserve judgment to see if my words would come to pass.

After arriving home, I received a call from the owner of TCT, a television station in Illinois, to appear on his station and release the same information. Because of where the station is situated, many of the viewers had voted for Gore and were upset and angry over the controversy. Some churches were divided because of the issue. After sharing the video, the prophetic information and the points concerning the will of God and the will of the people, many called and were steeled in their spirit that God was somehow going to direct this issue. They agreed with me that there was a reason for the "spiritual battle" over this election.

Since the election was over, I was not promoting one candidate over another. I was simply using the information found in the patterns and explaining them to the viewers.

While I was taping these programs, another call came from LESEA Broadcasting, another leading Christian network. They offered to fly their plane and pick me up to appear live on their daily program the following morning. I was not prepared for the trip and turned them down. I did a special five-minute videotape, and again shared that the patterns revealed that Bush would be the 43rd President of the United States.

After returning home, it struck me that if Bush was not elected and the recount decisions in Florida were overturned, I would look like a fool before the hundreds of thousands of people who had heard me speak. For some reason, I was not afraid to speak prophetically about this issue. I kept going back in my mind to the strange incident when we saw Governor Bush in Israel. What would be the chances of that happening?

When the U. S. Supreme Court finally settled the issue and the news commentators announced Bush was officially the 43rd President of the United States, my wife and I both cried. Emotionally, it was like a long journey that had finally come to an end. For some reason God had connected my spirit to this season in American history, and especially to the president.

Imagine my surprise when, on Christmas Day, my son and wife were waiting downstairs with a gift. Pam said, "This will probably be the most unusual and special gift you have received or may ever receive." It was a large photograph of me shaking hands with Bush in Israel. The picture was personally signed by the new President with the words, "To Perry–Best Wishes, G. W. Bush."

As the controversy around the outcome of the election continued, no one knew that America would soon be thrust into the most important war in her young history. Neither did I realize that a vision given to me in 1996 would come to pass.

Vision of the Five Tornadoes

The Bible indicates that the Holy Spirit would be the Agent bringing spiritual dreams, visions and revelation in the end-time:

> And it shall come to pass afterward that I will pour out My Spirit on all flesh; your sons and your daughters shall prophesy, your old men shall dream dreams, your young men shall see visions (Joel 2:28).

Receiving warnings and instruction from the Lord through a vision or a dream is nothing new in our family. For many years my father, Fred Stone, has been especially blessed to see events before they happen. This is not a "physic gift," but a special ability given to those who earnestly pray. Through the avenue of dreams and visions, Dad has seen wars before they happened and the assassination of world leaders months before they occurred. Through two different dreams, the life of his brother, Lewis Stone, was spared while Lewis was fighting in Vietnam.

Throughout the Bible, men received inspirational dreams. Jacob, who was later named Israel, was a dreamer (Genesis 28:12). His youngest son, Joseph, received the same gift and was exalted by Pharaoh in Egypt because of his ability to interpret strange dreams (Genesis 37:6-10). Perhaps this is a gift from the Lord, handed down from one generation to another.

A spiritual dream often employs symbolism that can be difficult to interpret (Daniel 7:15; 10:1). One such vision that I shared publicly for five years left me puzzled about the interpretation until the morning of September 11, 2001.

THE DARK TOWER AND THE FIVE TORNADOES

In June 1996, a colleague, Don Channell, and I were ministering at the Brooksville Assembly of God in Brooksville, Florida. After the morning service we enjoyed a meal in the home of our hosts. Feeling exhausted, I excused myself and went to the bedroom to lie down. As I was lying stomach-down on the bed, with an open Bible, I was overwhelmed with a sense of weariness. Instead of reading, I lay my cheek on the Bible.

In a matter of seconds, I felt myself moving through the blackness of space. Suddenly, a full-color, three-dimensional vision was before me. It was so real I could feel the wind and breathe the air. All five of my physical senses were active, yet I also understood I was lying on the bed. It was a strange sensation.

In this vision, I was standing at the bottom of a hill. Before me was a paved highway with sidewalks of concrete on both sides of the road. Houses lined the sidewalks. The homes were modest, comfortable and very neat. All of them were made of red brick. For some reason I sensed these homes were retired ministers who lived on Social Security.

I began walking up the hill on the left sidewalk. I recall wearing a suit, but had no shoes on my feet. Thinking this was odd, I continued up the hill. At the top of the hill there was a barrier—a large, five-foot concrete wall. I could barely see above the concrete wall, but noticed the striking, clear-blue sky without a cloud anywhere. Still walking, I looked up to observe a strange black object in the center of the sky that appeared as a large, black square. I recall thinking, "What a strange-looking cloud. It looks like the top of a building."

I finally reached the top of the hill and climbed on the concrete wall to see what was on the other side. I was awestruck and fearful of what I observed before me. Directly below was a beautiful, lush corn field. The golden tassels glowed with rich color on top of the corn. From my left to my right, as far as the eye could see, was row after row of beautiful corn. Everything seemed perfect—except for something at the end of the field, directly in front of me.

About 300 yards away I saw a large building that looked like the World Trade Center in New York City, except it had no windows. The scene was shrouded in a totally black cloud, and I realized this was the top of the building I had previously seen. The next scene was extremely frightening. Five tornadoes, in a perfect line, appeared to be spinning off of the large, black tower building.

The tornado on the left side was beginning to make a whooshing sound. It started spinning from the left to the right, in front of the dark tower that was in the center. Suddenly, red sparks of fire began shooting off of the first tornado that was spinning. I noticed that when the first tornado began to spin, it set the second one in motion—then the third, followed by the fourth and finally the fifth.

I knew what was about to happen. I knew the five tornados would come, one after the other. Each tornado would spin through the field, taking out a row of corn, then stop at the concrete barrier. The second storm would do the same, followed by the third, the fourth and the fifth. The area where a tornado hit was devastated, but the rest of the cornfield remained untouched as though nothing had happened.

In the distance near the power lines leading to the tower and a few feet from the concrete barrier, I saw a concrete water cistern, filled with water. I knew this cistern was the water source for the field. Since it was close to the barrier, I was uncertain if the water supply would be affected by the third tornado, or if the concrete where I stood would be enough to protect it.

In the vision I jumped from the concrete wall and headed down the hill, running at full speed. I was saying to myself, *The storms are coming, I must get to the cleft of the rock.* I repeated this twice and suddenly came out of the vision. My heart felt as though it would beat out of my chest. My breathing was heavy. I immediately jumped from the bed, ran down the hall to Don Channell's room and told him of the vision. Neither of us knew the meaning, but we knew it meant a sudden, unexpected series of storms that would instigate some type of damage.

FIVE MONTHS LATER

I shared the vision with several close friends and family members. Needless to say, I was greatly troubled. I felt the building was the World Trade Center. I felt that some form of terrorist attack would strike the building, resulting in great global economic storms. In fact, I publicly stated in several of my meetings that this could be the meaning of the vision.

Five months later, in a deep sleep I experienced a night vision (Daniel 2:19). This time I was in a major city. People were running down the aisles screaming, "The storm is coming, the storm is coming." I recall watching the crowd run into a large, downtown church constructed with grey, light-colored stones, not brick. We all went inside, and I remember seeing Asians, Hispanics, and African-Americans huddled in ethnic groups, hugging and praying. Everyone was fearful and expressed a look of dismay and shock. As they began to pray I counted five large tornadoes spinning outside the building. I thought the storm would be so strong that it would shake the church building off its foundation. The entire city felt the shaking, but the church remained intact. Looking through an opening where there should have been a door, I saw tons of paper and other objects spinning in the tornadoes. Five large tornadoes blew past the door, and then there was silence. Slowly, people began to exit the church. Outside, I could see debris scattered on the roads and sidewalks.

People were stunned and dazed. I looked around the city and saw one large skyscraper that was intact from the outside; but when I looked through the glass I could see that every office, computer, desk and filing cabinet throughout the entire building was useless. The structure was intact, but the inside of the building and its contents were ruined. On the street just below the building that was damaged internally, I saw piles of clothing, cans of food and in one area of the sidewalk, a small pile of children's toys. I thought it strange that the food and clothing were on the street and not distributed inside a building.

The dream ended after I walked toward a church building and saw five grey pearls scattered on the ground. I picked up the pearls one at a time, and began to string them back together on a string. Then I awoke. I immediately remembered the vision of the five tornadoes five months earlier, and felt that the first vision and this dream were one. Yet, I was very troubled about the dream and had no clear interpretation to the meaning. As days turned into weeks and weeks into months, I was reminded of Daniel praying for the understanding of a vision he was having difficulty interpreting.

In the third year of Cyrus, king of Persia, a message was revealed to Daniel, whose name was called Belteshazzar. The message was true, but the appointed time was long (Daniel 10:1).

It Was Reported on National Television

In February 1999, our ministry hosted a prophetic conference from our headquarters in Cleveland, Tennessee. The Daystar

Christian Television Network aired the conference live via satellite. I showed the viewers three drawings, an artist's rendition, of the visions from 1996. They included the black tower, the cornfield, the five storms blowing past the church and the large building in the city with the damage on the inside (see photos in this book).

With Y2K coming, I told them that my personal computer programmer said the dark tower could represent an older computer mainframe, and the five tornadoes could be five weeks or five months or even five years of storms. I concluded by telling the audience I was uncertain of the meaning of the vision and dream, but I believe we would know in the future if it was Y2K-connected or not.

The arrival of January 1, 2000, saw little or no impact on society. I told someone, "The tower must represent the World Trade Center. I don't understand it all, but something will happen in the future because this was a true vision, and not just a strange dream." I placed the series of pictures drawn by the local artist in my office closet, where they remained for 18 months.

On September 5, 2001, I was clearing the closet and found the pictures. I laid them on my office desk. I took the picture with the black tower and the cornfield into our Manna-Fest television room. I told Mel Colbeck, one of our workers, "See this picture? It hasn't happened yet, but I believe it will be a terrorist attack on the World Trade Center." Walking back into my office, I thought, *I may as well put these away for good after five years and nothing has clearly happened.*

September 11, 2001

On the morning of September 11th, I was working in our television mail room when the receptionist rushed in, saying, "I just got a phone call that a plane has hit the World Trade Center." I ran into my office and grabbed the picture. *This could be it . . . this could be the beginning of the five storms*, I thought. Soon a second worker came in saying, "Someone called and said a second plane has hit, and both towers are on fire!"

When she said "towers," I looked at the three-year-old picture and the black-looking tower. I screamed, "Oh my, that's it! The towers are burning with black smoke, that's why the tower looked black in the vision!" Rushing home, I turned on the news. Seeing the black smoke covering the *top* of the buildings, I said to my two colleagues standing beside me, "This is it. I saw the top of the building black, before I saw the five tornadoes. Five storms will come from this!"

Within 24 hours, both towers and five World Trade Center buildings were directly affected by the attacks. As sparks of fire fell from the twin towers, I realized this was why I saw sparks of fire spinning from the first tornado, setting the others on fire. In the dream, I saw tons of paper spinning inside the clouds. When the grey clouds of dust (which looked like, and was described as, tornadoes) settled, piles of paper were lying throughout the streets of New York. In the vision, as the storms raged people were headed into an old stone church to pray.

Weeks later, I was informed that Trinity Church, a church where George Washington prayed before he was inaugurated, was filled with people running from the disaster. They poured into the church to pray. The old church is a landmark and is built with stone and not brick, just as in my dream.

Later still, the announcement was made that several buildings were unsafe and the office equipment was ruined. This is the reason I saw entire structures intact, but the insides of the buildings unusable. The explanation of the vision and dream continued to be self-explanatory as the days passed.

The evening news reported that volunteers were placing clothes and food on the sidewalks for victim's families and workers. They even handed out toys to the children. I sat and wept.

Imagine the shock when I read an intelligence report months later indicating that the F.B.I. had discovered that this plot was planned five years before. This was about the same time the Lord had given me the first vision. My heart skipped when I later discovered some of the very terrorists had been staying less than an hour down the road from the very place the vision occurred.

FURTHER INTERPRETATION OF THE VISION AND DREAM

I believe these visions were fulfilled in part, beginning September 11, 2001. Let me explain:

- *Being barefoot* implies to be unprepared. It seems that no one was prepared for this event.

- *The left sidewalk* could allude to trouble. In the Bible the "left hand of God" represents trials and difficulty (Job 23:9). The first tornado came from the left side, representing the side of tragedy and trouble.

- *The homes were made of stone*, representing building on the rock, Jesus Christ (Matthew 7:24).

- *The homes* were homes of ministers. The street in front of the Trade Center complex is called Church Street. The large concrete wall could have alluded to Wall Street.

- *The black tower* was the World Trade Center, covered with the smoke from the attack. I did not see two towers, but if you stood in a certain area, the two were the same size and could appear as one building.

- *The five tornadoes contained fire*, referring to the attacks themselves that resulted in planes and fuel burning.

- *The tornadoes came in a series*, one after the other. Once the two towers were afire, five other buildings (Trade Center buildings 3, 4, 5, 6 and 7) were eventually destroyed.

- *The corn can represents the world economy or the harvest (Matthew 13:38).

♦ These *storms will impact the field in certain areas* but not the entire field.

♦ The *three ethnic groups* are a large part of the population in New York.

♦ People were *turning to the church and to prayer*. This literally happened throughout New York.

♦ *The building that was intact but ruined on the inside* represented buildings in New York where the structures were intact but the dust from the destruction went inside the buildings, making it impossible to use the computers, desks or furniture.

♦ *The clothes, food and toys on the sidewalks* and street are clearly the clothes and food being sent for relief workers and those in need.

♦ *The five grey colored pearls* represent the gospel, the "pearl of great price" (Matthew 13:46). The storm had scattered the pearls; but after the five storms, the five pearls were all on one necklace. In the vision I was standing in front of a church, when I put the the pearls back together.

The attack that brought the towers down lasted less than an hour. The tornadoes took out five rows of corn, in sequence, one after the other. In the Bible the field can represent the world, as Jesus said in Matthew 13:38.

Corn in the Bible represents prosperity. When the Bible speaks of the corn and wine it alludes to times of prosperity (Genesis 27:28). Corn and wine are called the fatness of the earth (Genesis 27:28). When the famine hit the world, the corn was affected and only the Egyptians had provision, because the king listened to a wise young Hebrew named Joseph (Genesis 41-44).

The fact is, both visions came to pass in minute detail. In the first vision, while running down the hill, I cried out, "The storms are coming, I must get to the cleft of the rock." The Rock is Christ and the cleft represents being hidden in his presence (1 Corinthians 10:4). We must turn to God and Christ since various storms will follow in the future.

The sovereign will of Almighty God is playing a role in preparing for the great fulfillment of many Biblical prophecies. By declaring war on terrorism, the door of end-time Bible prophecy has gone from a crack to a wide opening! This is because America is dealing with radical Islamic groups scattered around the globe who have their own prophetic agenda. We have stepped into the ring to battle with an invisible force, the same force that will energize a final dictator the Bible calls the Antichrist.

WHY BUSH OVER GORE?

President Bush was the right choice for the war on terror. His patience and resolve to take the conflict to the region of the world where our enemies were planning future attacks was the right choice.

Several Jewish friends from Israel pointed out to me that if Gore had been elected, we would have a Jewish Vice President, Joe Lieberman. Mr. Lieberman is a fine, upstanding and religious person. Since he is Jewish, however, the Islamic nations would have resisted any attempt from the United States to allow our troops on their soil. Our involvement would have been considered a movement by the Zionists to seize Muslim-controlled countries.

Insiders close to Bush say he spends quality time reading devotional material and praying for guidance and wisdom. I would much rather trust a man who places his confidence in God than a man whose decisions are made according to the opinion polls.

LESSONS I HAVE LEARNED IN THESE EXPERIENCES

- ◆ God can reveal the future to the most unsuspecting person there is.

- God will always confirm His revelation to you through circumstances and people around you.

- God will open a door to meet important people throughout your lifetime. Walk through these doors.

- You will almost never know why God revealed something until after the event happens.

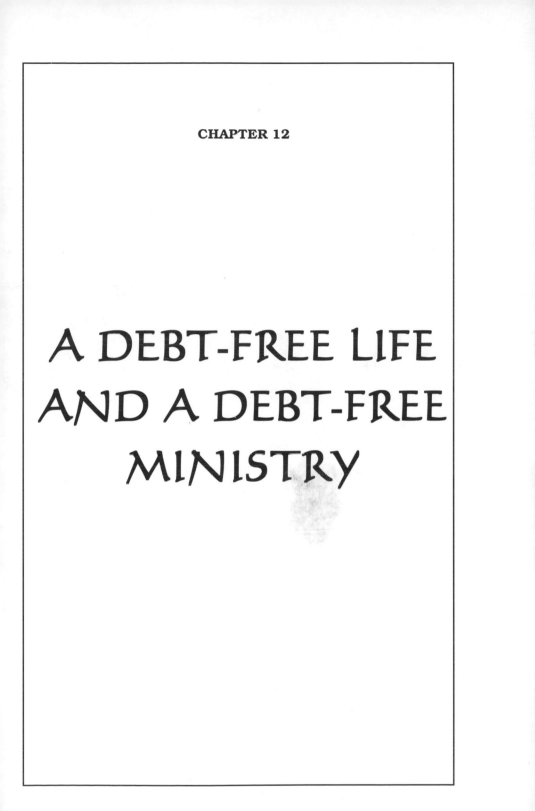

CHAPTER 12

A DEBT-FREE LIFE AND A DEBT-FREE MINISTRY

Owe no one anything except to love one another, for he who loves another has fullfilled the law (Romans 13:8).

A DEBT-FREE LIFE AND A DEBT-FREE MINISTRY

Two scriptures are foundational for our ministry, from a business perspective. Romans 12:11 tells us not to be slothful in business but be fervent in spirit, serving the Lord. The second one, in 13:8, tells us to owe no one anything but to love him.

From the outset of our ministry I prayed that the Lord would allow us to operate debt-free. In the past, many ministries began in the Spirit but ended up in the flesh. The leadership would birth an Ishmael instead of an Isaac. When you birth a promise from God (Isaac), then God will provide for the promise. When you birth Ishmael (your own plans), it will take all of your strength in the flesh to keep Ishmael alive!

Some ministries use the success principles of others in hopes that the results will be repeated for them. The ministry becomes method-oriented, going from one method or idea to another instead of birthing its own vision. Since my youth I have seen the church bus phase (every pastor purchased a church bus); the sports phase (we attracted people by forming a softball team); the home cell-group phase (stop Sunday night service and have cell groups), and the technology ministry phase (we must have a television ministry).

I tell local pastors that unless God calls you to preach to the world, your television program should reach the people in your area who can attend your church. Otherwise, you will be receiving email, letters and phone calls from other sheep and you will be a long-distance pastor. Purchasing air time for a national program is expensive and time-consuming. Some ministers have stepped out in faith and fallen down in failure. The bills for airtime and equipment begin to pile up and they are under continual stress to provide funds to pay them.

For these reasons, we have operated a debt-free ministry as much as possible. Usually we raise funds or set aside the money in advance before we begin a project. If we know a large bill will be coming due at a certain time, then we will watch our spending and set aside what is needed to pay the bill. When a ministry is smaller it has fewer bills to pay, but it also has fewer funds from which to draw. The larger a ministry grows, the more challenges it has. It works like this:

1. You begin in a small office with minimal payments that you are able to make.
2. The ministry outreach grows, and you need to hire some help.
3. Soon you are out of space, and need another office to accommodate growth.
4. The ministry outreach grows, and more staff is needed.
5. Soon your are out of storage and work space. You need a new building for the growth.

6. The ministry outreach grows, and more staff is needed

7. Soon you are out of storage and work space, and you need a larger facility.

These growth cycles produce non-stop birthing pains. Our ministry has worked from an apartment, the basement of a house, a one-room office, a 2,000-square-foot office, a 7,800-foot office, a 25,000 square-foot office and now another 45,000-square-foot facility. This process has continued since 1982. Just when we think we can settle in, it is time to build again!

Why Operate Debt-Free?

Maintaining a debt-free ministry is important for many reasons. If you pastor a church you will discover some members are "field hoppers." They will feed in your pasture and eventually head across town to a greener field. Your income can shift not only by members jumping the fence, but according to the availability of jobs and income in your region. There are times when some folks will split off from the flock and "do their own thing." If there are unexpected changes and you are in heavy debt, then you as a leader will carry a daily burden.

An evangelist has no guarantee of a steady income. If he is physically unable to minister for an extended time, his income can drop and circumstances can be detrimental to him and his family. If a minister preaches something controversial he can lose support before sunrise. A church operates from tithes and an evangelist lives off of offerings. When there is an economic downturn, faithful members continue to tithe, but often withhold special offerings. For this reason we choose to operate, when possible, a debt-free ministry.

The Strange Key to Being Debt-Free

It has been said, "What you cause to happen to others, God will cause to happen for you." This was demonstrated to us in 1997 when we were preparing to build our ministry center on Michigan Avenue Road. That year, our 7,800-square-foot ministry office was packed to capacity. Boxes lined the walls going in and out of the offices. There was no available space for additional storage. With each new book we printed an entire day was spent securing storage space. One afternoon I sensed an urgency in my spirit to tell Pam to get in the van and drive around town.

When I went into her office, I said, "We must leave now!" She sat there, and said, "Okay. Where are we going?" I told her the Lord was putting it in my heart to drive around town and look for some office space or some land.

I had been looking for a large building for six months and had given up. We began driving and ended up on Michigan Avenue Road, a section of town I had never been in. As we topped a hill, nestled below us was a beautiful piece of property. It was about 14 acres with an old white house and two old barns on the hill. The real estate sign said, "For Sale: Contact Max Carroll." I almost jumped out of the van. Max is the brother of Ralph Carroll, who served on my board of directors! I was drawn to the property like a magnet. A feeling of serenity and peace came over me. I instructed Pam to write down the number and call Max for more details.

The property was listed for $220,000. It was worth the price, but higher than I felt we could afford. I asked Max, "Would you call the family and tell them a ministry wants to buy it? See if they could come down some on the price."

"That may be good and it may be bad" he responded. "Not everyone is excited about ministries purchasing property, but it won't do any harm to ask."

Within days, Max called and said one of the members of the family wanted to meet with me. We met at the property. He was a very friendly and kind gentleman who began to ask me about my ministry and my plans for the property. I shared with him my desire to build a studio, to have a place to produce our resource material, and have offices where people could order material and call in for prayer. I also mentioned we had a missions ministry. When I said "missions" I saw his face light up.

"What kind of missions?" He asked.

"I travel some overseas to preach large soul-winning meetings, and I support missionaries who carry the gospel to various nations of the world."

Missions was the word! The man began to tell me a story. He pointed to the old run-down, white frame house on the hill. "That's the house I was raised in," he said, reminiscing. "My mother was a Christian, she was a dedicated Baptist. She always wanted to go to the mission field and she loved missionaries. She won a fellow to the Lord one time who became a missionary. She would sit in a chair on the porch, overlooking this field where we are standing, and pray for the missionaries!"

My heart pounded with excitement. The property had been covered with prayer years ago! It was blessed by someone who loved souls and evangelism. The man said, "I will talk to the family and get back with you." I left and told Pam, "That property is marked for the gospel!"

A few days later a call came from Max. "Perry, you won't believe this. The family had a meeting and said they know of nothing better they had rather see on this property than a building for winning souls. Not only that, they want to offer it to you for $180,000, which is $40,000 less than what they were initially asking!" "Tell them it is sold!" I shouted.

I Saw it Eight Years Before

After signing the papers for the land, I would drive around it and pray. There was something about the house on the hill, but I couldn't quite put the puzzle in my spirit together. One day I parked in the large field and walked up the hill, through the high weeds, toward the white house. Suddenly I saw it. A set of concrete steps covered with weeds was in front of the white house. I looked behind me and saw where we would build the new television studio. I was standing on a paved road separating the field from the hill. In front of me was the house with the old concrete steps leading to the door.

I began to shout and scream, "Oh Lord, that is it!" It was the exact property I saw in the night vision in Leeds, Alabama, eight years before. There was the paved road, a small hill and concrete steps. The man was standing at a television tower. He was actually standing where the white house sat. My mind raced and my spiritual imagination began to reason, "Was the man in the night vision a guardian angel linked to the praying woman? Had the angel marked this property for God?" Then I said, "What we are going to accomplish on this property must be connected to global evangelism and reaching people through television."

Again, my sweetheart was the first person to hear it. "Pam, it's the same property I saw in Leeds in 1988!" Pam is so level-headed, she doesn't get overly excited about anything—except a good family vacation! She smiled and said, "Praise God." I felt like throwing her in the air and saying, "Hey, hey! Attention, please! This is a major thing." However, she looked at me as if to say, "Why are you so shocked that the Lord is directing you?"

A Million Dollars Short

After architects drew plans and the steel was ordered for the new 25,000-square-foot office and studio, the ministry was about a million dollars short. One million is a large number, but it may as well been five million because we didn't have the money. Two times during major building projects I sent a letter inviting people to plant a special offering, but I knew from the past that we couldn't raise more than $50,000 by asking directly. It would have to come from a supernatural source. I began to pray for a miracle. I also knew that often we must act on our faith to initiate God's miracle. The miracle process began during a Sunday night service at World Harvest Church in Columbus, Ohio.

The Treasure of Your Heart

Randy White, ministering at World Harvest Church in Columbus, Ohio, invited Charlie Ellis and me to be in the service. That Sunday night Randy began ministering on "The Treasures of Your Heart." During the message people began to run from the audience to the altar and lay offerings on the steps. Some began bringing jewelry and others went to their cars to bring objects of value and lay them on the altar. The funds raised that night were going to help World Harvest build a youth center.

Standing in the second row I heard the still, small voice I had heard throughout my ministry saying, "What is the treasure of your heart?" I pondered, then thought, *My family*! The question came again, "What do you have that you could give to the church as a seed offering?" In a flash my mind went to a sports card collection I had purchased for a few thousand dollars. According to the seller, it was worth about $40,000. I intended to sell it in the future for my son's education or some other important event.

The Holy Spirit impressed me to give this entire collection to the World Harvest Ministries. The Lord spoke to my spirit and said, "Give to this ministry to use for their ministry, and you will dedicate your building debt-free." I ran to the front and whispered into the ear of Pastor Parsley, "I am going to send you a valuable card collection for my miracle."

I returned home, packaged about 17 boxes of cards and shipped them to World Harvest Ministries. I felt a peace and a release in my spirit. I told Pam what the Lord had spoken to me, and a few curious staff workers asked me what in the world I was doing, packing up all those cards. This act of obedience initiated the first in a series of miracles.

A few days later, a woman from Florida called and said, "The Lord has impressed me to send you a donation for your new ministry facility." I thanked her and told her she could mail the check to the ministry. She replied, "I may need to deliver this one myself." When she arrived with her husband and handed me a check for $50,000, my first thought was, "That covered the cards I gave away!" This was the largest donation we had ever received. Now we needed another $950,000! But my faith was now sparked by this unexpected miracle. As we began to build, we would experience a breakthrough just in time to pay the bills.

Those "Hidden Cards"

As contractors worked on the new ministry facility, Pam and I continued to travel and minister in churches. I was preaching on "Windows 98" at Brooksville, Florida, in the spring. Suddenly, the Lord brought something to my attention that momentarily stunned me. I remembered that there were two or three boxes of rookie cards in the closet of our guest bedroom at home. Those cards were a part of the original set I sent to World Harvest months before. I knew I must send those remaining cards for the Promise of God to be fulfilled concerning my own ministry center being debt-free.

I stopped preaching, looked at Pam on the front row and said, "Write this down: send cards." When I said this, Pastor Dave Garcia stood to his feet and walked out of the building. I thought nothing of it until after the altar service. Pastor Garcia handed me a check for the revival offering. He made a statement to the church that when I said something to Pam, the Lord spoke to him to give an additional $10,000 from their building fund for our new ministry center. The moment I obeyed the Lord to follow through with the cards, the Lord impressed the pastor to sow a special financial gift into the ministry! He knew nothing about the cards or the word the Lord had given me about dedicating the building debt-free.

We began the building with a pay-as-you-go concept. We would get low on funds, and something unexpected would happen. Late into spring we were two months from the planned building dedication. I was preparing for a trip to Africa when the contractor came and said, "We will need $200,000 to complete the project. I need half now, and half when the building is finished." At that moment I began to waver. I called my banker and requested a loan for $200,000. I knew this was breaking my pattern of operating debt-free, but I thought, *Well, the Lord has helped us, and I haven't told but a handful about what the Lord told me, so if it doesn't happen, God and I won't be embarrassed!* The President of the bank told me he could get me $100,000 now and $100,000 when I returned from Africa. I agreed and headed to Kenya, West Africa, to minister at the great Lighthouse Church.

Another Word of Confirmation

During the first service in Africa, the praise and worship team began singing and the old soccer stadium began to bounce with joy as over 4,000 people sent high praises into heaven. As the pastor directed the worship using a guitar and a microphone, his song turned into a prophetic word. The Holy Spirit was encouraging the people.

Then these words came forth, "Thus saith the Lord, I am with you and will direct you. You don't need a bank loan." I could have fallen out cold on the concrete. He knew nothing about my situation. The missionary with me began to shout at me, "The Lord is talking to you and you know it!" I called Pam from Africa and said, "I don't know how I am going to do it, but cancel the second bank loan." I returned from Africa inspired and ready to complete the assignment.

The building dedication was set for Saturday, May 15. That week we conducted a special meeting in Cleveland and invited our partners to the dedication. When I went to bed that night I owed $100,000 on the building. I remember lying down in the guest room, wanting to be by myself because I wasn't feeling well. I said aloud, "Okay, Lord. I appreciate what You have done, but I am glad I didn't tell everyone what You told me because we would both be embarrassed!" As I complained, the Lord reminded me that His promise was, "You will dedicate your building debt-free on dedication day."

The word *on* began to resonate in my spirit. Tomorrow was the day. What did God have planned *on* dedication day? Time would tell!

One of the Great Miracles of Our Ministry

Over 350 partners and friends packed the large room that would house the new studio, to dedicate the 25,000-square-foot ministry center. Just before we cut the ribbon I shared my heart and told the people we were just $100,000 short from paying off the building. Pam handed me several checks in an envelope that morning and I said, "Some of our partners sent in an offering for the building." As I went through the checks one was $10,000, another was $5,000, and Pam and I were sowing $2,000. I said, "Well, praise God, we have $17,000!"

Suddenly, some in the audience indicated they had prepared a special offering for the building dedication. I announced, "If you already have an offering prepared, then you can bring it to the front." I was amazed as hundreds literally stood to their feet and lined up to give an offering they had already prepared to give. I told Pam to get a calculator and begin counting the offering while we walked outside to the main entrance to cut the yellow ribbon.

About 30 minutes later she ran into my office with a bright smile and a twinkle in her eye. She handed me a paper with the total. It read $102,000! The building was paid in full at the very moment we were cutting the ribbon and bringing our partners into the lobby area.

Later, as we enjoyed lunch in the studio, there was a mist of light visible a few feet from the ceiling. Those present began to rejoice and say, "We believe it is the glory of the Lord!" The Lord knew my heart was to operate a debt-free ministry, and He demonstrated to me His supernatural ability to fulfill his promise.

The ministry center complex dedicated that day is now filled and overflowing with resource material, television equipment and office personnel. The ministry is expanding with a new 45,000-square-foot facility. The growth continues and we are still expanding, because we are not finished yet.

Lessons I Have Learned in These Experiences

- ◆ The borrower is always a servant to the lender.
- ◆ A worldwide ministry must operate with the same wisdom a normal business does.
- ◆ God often requires you to sow to someone else in order for someone to sow to you.
- ◆ It is God's best to operate debt-free. This enables you to remain free from excessive cares of life.
- ◆ God will use others to make happen for you what you help make happen for others.

CHAPTER 13

KINGDOM CONNECTIONS, SPECIAL FRIENDS

A man who has friends must himself be friendly, but there is a friend who sticks closer than a brother (Proverbs 18:24).

KINGDOM CONNECTIONS, SPECIAL FRIENDS

In Genesis 1, at the time of Creation, God scanned the earth after six days of creative activity and announced six times, "That's good." The fish in the sea, the fowls in the air, the variety of flowers and the lush trees in the garden were set in perfection. God created Adam and placed him in this garden paradise to "keep the garden."

Adam was given the assignment of naming all the creatures God had created. This was a huge task, since there are over 500,000 species of animal life on earth. After completing this mission, God looked at Adam and saw one thing in His entire creation that He declared was not good.

God said, "It is not good that man should be alone" (Genesis 2:18). God created for Adam a helper, a helpmate. God knew that a dog, a cat or other pet was not the same as a loving human being who could build a physical relationship with Adam.

You and I were created for friendships and relationships. God is love; and when a person is loving and affectionate, he or she must share his feelings with others. God created the angels for fellowship. Afterward he formed Adam and called him "the son of God" (Luke 3:38). Later, the Almighty created a nation unto Himself called Israel; He called Israel "my son" (Hosea 11:1). Hundreds of years later, Christ came to earth and was called the "son of God" (Luke 1:35). Those who receive Christ as their Lord and Savior are called the "sons of God!"

Apparently, God desires intimate relationships so that He can bond with His creation. When people do not form friendships and relationships, they are not fulfilling the purpose for which they were created. Our greatest treasures in life are our family and the friends we make along the journey. Without friends, life would become routine and rather boring. Without the fellowship and relationship of people we enjoy and love, life would be lonely. It is not good for man to be alone. A man or a woman must have friends.

Friendships lead to partnerships. A partner is someone who believes in your assignment, has caught your vision. It is someone who desires to link their faith and finances with you to reach the same goal. In ministry, partners are those who support the ministry through prayer and giving. Pastor Jentezen Franklin calls these individuals "Kingdom Connections."

The church today has become a fast-food buffet feeding center where the people walk in, sit down, eat a quick bite, leave a few dollars for the tip (offering), and get out of the building before the Amen is said. We have lost the gift of building relationships within the church because everyone is too busy with their own assignments to link their time with others. We must get back to building relationships with others of similar, precious faith. Your destiny and future assignment is always linked with someone else.

In retrospect, I can see where God placed three special friends in my life when I was a teenager, who would help impart into my own future assignment.

THE TALE OF THREE FRIENDS

Perhaps you have heard the names Jentezen Franklin, Randy White and Marcus Lamb. I have been personal friends with these three men for many years. We are all from the same denomination, the Church of God. We were all raised by outstanding Christian parents. We were all called to preach in our early teens and began ministering as teenagers. We were all involved in attending youth camps and camp meetings. We all married women who make *us* look good! The early friendships among these three ministers set the stage for what would become an amazing link for our future destinies. The story begins with Marcus Lamb.

THE YOUNG MARCUS LAMB

Marcus was from Macon, Georgia. He completed High School at age 14 and by age 15 was attending Lee College in Cleveland, Tennessee. By age 18, Marcus was traveling across the nation, conducting extended revivals in local churches of various denominations. He was known as the "Walking Bible," often quoting hundreds of scriptures a night when preaching.

I saw his picture in the church's state paper, announcing that he would be preaching a summer youth camp in Virginia. I determined to attend the meeting and become acquainted with Marcus and his ministry. Marcus would often sport a white suit, and always had the moustache that marks him to this day. He could preach the paint off the wall, and quoted so many scriptures you thought his brain was actually linked to a computer hard drive featuring Bible software! The altar results were astonishing with hundreds being saved and filled with the Holy Spirit.

We were both teenagers, and I was beginning to have extended meetings. Church leaders were whispering that Marcus and I might one day be high-level executives in the denomination, if we remained faithful to our call and to the church. We certainly were not seeking any position, but were both consumed with having revivals and winning souls. Staying in touch over the telephone and through the mail, Marcus would often share with me the results of a meeting where he was preaching and encourage the pastor to invite me for a revival.

Two Humorous Incidents

As teenagers we attended the General Assembly in Dallas, Texas. I drove to the meeting and Marcus flew in. I requested that he select the hotel accommodations by phone. We could not afford the downtown hotels, and knew nothing about the city of Dallas. Arriving at the airport, he said, "We need to find the hotel. I made a lot of calls and found one that will be $195.00 for the week, but we will need to drive a few miles to get to the convention center."

We searched and finally came to the building the owner called a "hotel." The owner should have been arrested for false advertising. We were both shocked to discover the joint was actually one of those one-hour stop in and leave places (if you know what I mean). The atmosphere was scary, and the room was so raunchy that a portion of the ceiling was falling in and the beds had no sheets on them.

I could imagine my car being stripped of the tires and the engine while I was trying to sleep in this dump. We went to the "manager" and had to threaten him with the police to get our deposit back. We left the premises, drove around and finally found a Days Inn near the stadium.

During the meeting we attended the teen talent competition. It seemed Marcus had preached in every church and could tell you the minutest details about the pastor, the choir director, and even name the people competing in the choirs and solo division of the talent contest. A choir from Sumiton, Alabama, was competing. Marcus had just preached there, and knew many in the youth group. He invited a young lady to go eat after the service and she accepted. The problem was that I had the car and was the driver. I was not about to be a lonely chauffeur, driving him to eat! He suggested to the young lady that she find a female friend who would like to go with us, so I would not feel stupid driving him around.

That night we ate with the youth group and spent time fellowshiping with the group and the two young ladies. We eventually sent them back to where the choir was staying. I enjoyed the company of the young lady, and asked Marcus if it would be possible to get together with them for dinner.

The following day, Marcus came to me, looking rather pale, and said, "You won't believe this. I just found out that the girl you ate with last night was divorced only a short time ago. Had I known this, I would have never asked her to go." At the time we were both in shock. I could see my young reputation sinking as fast as the Titanic. I went into a moment of depression but within a few hours, we were back at the convention, having a wonderful time of fellowship. Without a doubt, the best thing to ever happen to Marcus and to me was when he met Joni and I met Pam!

THE TELEVISION STATION

Marcus eventually married Joni. Together they moved to Montgomery, Alabama, where they obtained a license for a Christian television station. I traveled to Montgomery to assist in an early telethon to raise funds for the station. Under the direction of the Holy Spirit, Marcus sold the station and moved to Dallas, where he invested in a station—KMPX, Channel 22—in Dallas.

I was honored to be the first guest Marcus had when he turned the power on in the Dallas-Fort Worth area. At 7 o'clock that evening, the Daystar Christian Network went on the air! There

was only one station and no viewing audience, so we did not receive many calls that first night. When I returned the next year,
the studio was a masterpiece and the phones were now ringing
steadily, as believers throughout the region began catching the
vision of Christian television in the area.

TWO STRANGE THINGS HAPPENED

On two separate occasions, bizarre things happened at the station. To us, it was a sign of spiritual warfare in heavenly places.
Marcus has said:

> Satan is the prince of the power of the air, and tele-
> vision sends signals into the air—the very stronghold
> of the enemy. Therefore it is not strange that when a
> ministry expands on television, they will hit very strong
> spiritual opposition.

One night I was teaching a revelation the Holy Spirit had given
me concerning the link of the Antichrist to the Islamic religion.
During an important point in my teaching, the lights in the entire studio went off. I was unsure if the television signal entering
the homes was gone or just the lights. In the darkness I heard
Marcus say, "The lights are out but the people at home can still
hear. Keep teaching."

We assumed that a huge storm had blown into the area and
damaged something. Later, we were informed that it was perfectly clear outside. After several minutes the lights returned.
Someone or something had cut the main power switch off in the
main power room! There was no one in the room and no one had
walked past the producers to enter the room.

I told Marcus, "The enemy did not want this message out over
the airwaves."

On a second occasion, I was preparing a prophetic message
that would reveal some important information to the public. I was
waiting in the studio set near a large table when suddenly I heard

a crashing sound: the frame of a large, hanging studio light had come loose and crashed about three feet from my head!

I had been sitting at the table and had just decided to stand for a moment. Had the heavy metal frame hit my head, it would have cracked or crushed my skull. The floor director said, "It would probably have killed you." He told me that nothing like that had ever happened before.

For several years, on the night I was scheduled to appear on any station, strange storms would brew from out of nowhere and knock down power lines. Several times the television transformers blew out for no logical reason, and we could not go live for the teaching session. Some stations began saying, "Well it looks like the old devil knows Perry is back in town!"

As I would teach and see the response of the people, as phones lines would jam and souls would come to the Lord, I understood two things. First, the power of television and secondly, the reason the bizarre attacks came was to stop the messages from being preached! Certainly Christian television pierces the darkness through the signals it sends into the atmosphere and by satellite.

THE DAYSTAR TELEVISION NETWORK

Marcus has remained faithful to God, to his family and to the call of God on his life. Today, the Daystar Television Network is the second largest Christian Network in America (TBN is the largest). The Daystar Network has numerous stations, and is aired on cable networks throughout North America. It is also carried on two overseas satellites. Our weekly program Manna-Fest is aired several times each week on the Daystar Network.

Marcus and I never imagined that our meeting as two teenage evangelists under the old tabernacle in Virginia would ever build such an interwoven friendship and destiny. Our relationship continues for the advancement of the kingdom of God.

JENTEZEN FRANKLIN, SAXOPHONE-PLAYING EVANGELIST

Two days after Pam and I were married, we drove our blue Buick, packed with clothes and my study materials, into the driveway of the parsonage at the Lynwood Church of God in Gastonia, North Carolina. Pastor Walter Mauldin had been Pam's pastor for several years, and was the pastor when I conducted the four-week revival where Pam and I met.

We were welcomed into the house as "the honeymooners." Every night for three weeks, Pastor Mauldin reminded the congregation this was a "honeymoon revival." It seemed everyone would cut their eyes to me sitting on the platform, and grin from the sides of their mouths.

During this revival I had a dream that proved to be prophetic. I dreamed I was in a large room with four doors. Each door had a sign attached to it and steps leading up to it. I was given a choice of entering only one door. Behind the first door were college kids. They seemed to be in a party spirit instead of an attitude of soberness. I knew in my mind that I would not choose this door.

I opened the second door and found a group of ministers wearing black suits—leaders of the denomination. I could join them and simply "follow the system," but I sensed no leading in this direction. The third door was a carnal door that had carnal pleasures behind it. Naturally, I rejected this door. The fourth door read "Persecution." Reluctantly, I chose this door.

As I walked up the steps, the door swung open and I saw the silhouette of large city. Suddenly, a strange-looking person shrouded in a tight black garment appeared with a sword and began swinging at me. I had a sword, and began fighting back. In one thrust I cut off the hand of the attacker and the hand holding the sword dropped to the ground. As I turned, another attacker was there, and I repeated the same method of stopping the assailant. This was repeated several times. I realized the secret of defeating these adversaries was the power of the sword.

The Lord spoke to me and said, "The amount of Word you know and use will determine the length of your sword." I knew he was referring to the Scripture as the "sword." He also said, "Blessed is the man who is skilled with the sword, he will not fall." I knew that Jesus overcame all temptation using the Word of God, which prevented him from falling into Satan's snare. At that moment I knew that my ministry would face times of severe persecution from people, but my endurance and ability to stand would be in the knowledge and use of God's Word! As the years pass, this interpretation certainly proves true.

It was also during this revival that a young, skinny, black-haired man stood on the church platform to minister and sing. His name was Jentezen Franklin. He and his brother, Richey, were beginning to travel and preach in local churches. Their father was serving as the evangelism director for the Church of God in Western North Carolina. I recall the humble and sincere spirit they both manifested.

As Jentezen began playing the saxophone and singing, I had never heard anyone more anointed on a musical instrument in my life. After the service I told Pam, "These young men will make an impact for God. I can feel it in my spirit!" During that meeting, Jentezen attended several services and years later said that, during the three-week revival, our ministry imparted an inspiration in his spirit to do more for God that just be an average minister.

Months later I began to hear that a young man from North Carolina was having outstanding revivals, and was a powerful pulpit preacher. His name was Jentezen Franklin. For several years, our paths crisscrossed while traveling the nation ministering in local churches. Pam and I began developing a close friendship with him and his lovely wife, Sherise.

AN ANGEL OF THE LORD

On several occasions Jentezen and I have traveled overseas together to minister. During one unforgettable trip, we flew with an interpreter to Budapest and took a vehicle into the former Communist Romania for a series of evangelistic meetings.

When we arrived, the posters announcing the meetings had been torn down and there was a division among the churches. The large hall was only half-filled, and the pastor was afraid of expressing too much emotion in the service. I felt greatly hindered in the spirit realm. Returning to the hotel, Jentezen and I were discussing the issue and talking about our families, which we were missing. We were sharing a double bedroom with simple accommodations.

Early in the morning and without warning, a presence came into the room that was so strong my hair stood on end. Jentezen felt it at the same time and said, "What is that?" The room became so illuminated that we could see pictures hanging on the wall that were previously not visible. Suddenly, the anointing overwhelmed us and we began shouting, praying and weeping. We both discerned the presence of an angel of the Lord coming to strengthen us. The presence lingered for about 30 minutes and then lifted.

That night the spiritual tide began to turn. For eight straight days we ministered in packed and overflowing auditoriums, and hundreds came to Christ. We could sense this special "presence" throughout our journey, until we arrived late at night at the Romanian-Hungarian border, then it lifted.

The worst part of the overseas trip was being away from our wives. I had been married about seven years, and Jentezen had been married only a few years and had never been away from his wife for a substantial length of time. When the meetings ended, we would have swam back across the ocean, almost, if we could have made it home sooner! Today we often laugh about when Jentezen went with me on an overseas trip and within a month after returning, his wife was pregnant. They have a family of four girls and one boy. His wife has instructed me to not take Jentezen with me on any more overseas trips!

THE DECISION THAT WOULD CHART HIS DESTINY

Several times, we both traveled to Israel. During one tour, I observed that Jentezen appeared to be restless in his spirit. I asked him if everything was okay. He shared with me, as his close friend, something that was greatly burdening him. Prior to the trip he had received a conference call from five of the denomination's main youth leaders. They were telling him that if he would do three things and remain faithful, he could "make it to the top." In fact they told him if he would follow their advice, they would help him get to the top ("the top" meant to be the national director of the Youth Ministries for the denomination).

I asked him, "What are the three things" He looked at me with a sad countenance, and said "I hate to even say it." I replied, "Go ahead." He said:

> They told me not to preach anything that is controversial. To stay with a basic message and stay away from any form of controversy. They then said for me not to be involved in being too "charismatic," or promote anything that looks like it is a part of the Charismatic Movement. Then they told me, "Don't be like Perry Stone. We don't need another Perry Stone, so don't be like him and you'll make it."

He turned his face and looked out the window of the bus. I began laughing. I said, "Listen Jent, God is blessing me and that doesn't bother me so don't let it bother you."

He replied, "It does bother me. I do not want men to push me or men to think they are controlling my ministry, or men getting credit for what God is doing. I am praying about pastoring a church that is not even in the denomination."

I told him, "Just do what God tells you to do and don't worry about what men say." At that moment I recalled the dream of the four doors. How strange that I had the dream in 1982, during the same revival where I had met Jentezen. Here was an example of "verbal persecution" from my fellow ministers. I had chosen this door, so I was not concerned about the negative opinion of others.

A few months later, I learned that Jentezen had become the pastor of the Free Chapel Worship Center in Gainesville, Georgia. Several denominational leaders warned him, "You are making a terrible mistake. You are ruining your future with the church." Despite these false alarms, Jentezen walked in obedience to God's word.

When it was time for one of his first revivals, I received the call to be the evangelist. What a powerful church! With 450 members, the congregation was alive with the anointing and zeal of the Lord. We conducted several revivals in the old sanctuary, to overflow crowds. Under Pastor Franklin, the church grew and the sanctuary was too small for the masses of people. He soon erected a large 2,500 seat sanctuary to accommodate the growth.

In May 1997, I was thrilled to conduct a five-week revival at the Free Chapel Worship Center. Each night the building was full, and the spiritual results were outstanding. Hundreds were saved and filled with the Holy Spirit. Today, Pastor Franklin is in a new 5,000 seat auditorium located off a main road in Gainesville. His television program, Kingdom Connections, is viewed around the world. The friendship that began between two "kid preachers" in North Carolina in 1982 has developed into a personal relationship as both make an impact for the kingdom of God today.

THE RANDY WHITE MIRACLE

The third close friend of this ministry is Randy White. Randy is a fifth generation minister who began ministering as a teenager. He too was impacted by the ministry of Dr. T.L. Lowery. In fact, Marcus, Jentezen, Randy and I are all considered "spiritual sons" of Dr. Lowery. Years ago, Randy was on staff at Dr. Lowery's church in Fort Washington, Maryland.

Randy laughingly tells the humorous story of when Brother Lowery's entire staff was on duty making final preparations for the dedication of a new church building. It was in 1988, and Pat Robertson was arriving on Sunday to dedicate the new facility. Randy said, "We literally stayed up three nights without sleep, sanding the sheetrock, painting the walls and setting up chairs." He recalls:

> On Saturday night at 3 o'clock in the morning, six hours before the doors opened for dedication, Pastor Lowery remembered we had forgotten to mow the grass around the church. It was November, but he wanted everything to look perfect. He instructed me to get the mower and a flashlight and cut the grass. There I was with three days of no sleep, holding a flashlight and pushing a lawn mower. However, everything *was* ready by 9 o'clock in the morning!

When I became acquainted with Randy, he had gone through something every minister dreams he will never have to experience, a divorce. Then, a divorced minister could not be ordained under any conditions, even if his wife had left him for another man. Because of certain circumstances, some ministers told Randy he was washed up and he may as well find a secular job. With a brilliant business mind, it was not difficult for him to obtain a job in the State Department. He even started several personal businesses. This was not God's plan for him, however, because the "gifts and calling of God are without repentance." His heart still yearned to minister and help the poor and needy.

One night in 1989, I was sitting with Randy in his car in front of a school building where I was preparing to minister. He was sharing his heart with me. Suddenly the Spirit of the Lord came over me and I spoke a prophetic word over his life. The Spirit said, "The rod of Aaron looks dead. It has no life in it, but the rod of Aaron will blossom again!" Aaron's rod was a dead tree branch, a simple stick with no life. When Aaron placed it at the door of the tabernacle where the Lord's presence dwelt, the presence of the Lord brought life to the rod and it began to produce almonds and leaves! The Holy Spirit was informing Randy that his ministry presently looked dead but was going to blossom again! We both began to cry and rejoice.

Several years later, I learned that he and Paula had moved to Tampa, Florida, and had started a church in a local elementary school. I received a call to preach his first revival in the newly-organized church. Pam, Jonathan and I traveled to Tampa for the meeting. At that time, Tampa was a spiritually wicked city. There was little impact of the gospel in the city; and strip joints, bars and drugs were the life of the town.

I was informed that the Mafia had moved out of the northern cities and relocated to Tampa to be closer to the coast where the drugs were coming into the country. Several kingpins of pornography had a dark grip on the city. While staying in the hotel, Jonathan would awake the same time every night and scream in torment as though someone was hurting him. There was a cloud of spiritual darkness covering the entire area.

Each night during the revival we set up equipment and, after service, broke down the room to prepare for school the next day. Randy had about 27 members. Our largest crowd was about 80 people. Randy had engaged every member in some form of ministry. There were greeters, parking attendants, ushers, musicians—everyone was doing something! He outgrew the school and purchased a warehouse, naming the church the South Tampa Christian Center. It, too, was located in a "rough" section of the city.

WITHOUT WALLS INTERNATIONAL CHURCH

Randy and Paula felt their ministry was for the "down and out," those rejected by society and who may not be accepted by the traditional church. They began taking church to the inner city projects by initiating a "Sidewalk Sunday School." The church began busing in the poor children and ministering to their parents. As they had pity for the poor, God was preparing to bless them with influence in the entire city.

After a few years at South Tampa, God provided a new location for a new church and ministry. Randy drove me to the new building he was interested in buying. The outside was in rough condition, but the interior looked like a bombed-out building in a war zone. As we toured the "wreckage," I knew he was wearing faith glasses to see this place as a major ministry office, because all I saw was a mess!

Through a series of amazing events and a last-minute $630,000 miracle, Randy purchased the four-story office complex that would be remodeled and become the headquarters of the future Without Walls International Church and the Paula White Ministries. Since they did not have a sanctuary, they hoisted a large 3,000-seat tent beside the office complex.

In March 1997, I preached a five-night camp meeting under the tent. It was the coldest week on record, and one night a storm hit the area. Strong men, including several of the players from the NFL Tampa Bay Buccaneers football team, were gripping the huge poles, attempting to hold them down to prevent the tent from collapsing on about 800 people.

One night while preaching in the tent, Randy was receiving the offering at the conclusion of the service. Suddenly, Paula came running down the aisle like she had seen a ghost. She grabbed Randy and said, "Someone has set the back of the tent on fire!" I caught a view of Pam at the book table and she was acting rather nervous, running around as though looking for someone or trying to escape. My first thought was, "This place is about to ignite and start a massive fire." I began to look for a door.

Randy smiled and continued with the offering. Paula looked like she could slap him on the head. The offering was received and Randy asked an usher if everything was okay. They affirmed it was. Service was dismissed and we headed to the conference room for a meal. Paula said, "Randy why didn't you get nervous? Someone outside had set the flaps on fire." He replied, "What you did not know was the fabric is fireproof! The city would never allow us to set up the tent without it being fireproof." Paula and Pam began laughing. Randy said, "The first law of dealing with something like this is, 'Don't let people see you sweat.'"

Pam and I feel we have a legacy with the Whites and their church. Randy has told me that, of all the speakers he hosts at Without Walls, our meetings bring in more people that stay with the church than any other speaker. Our early friendships set the pace for the longtime relationships we now enjoy!

Because of their influence and anointing, all of the above friends, Marcus, Jentezen and Randy, bear battle scars from various spiritual conflicts. However, Pam and I stick with our friends through thick and thin.

Friends and Special Influences

God places special people in your life for a reason. Individuals make either deposits or withdrawals from you. Some continually pull on your time and energy, while others are a joy to spend time and energy on. God places people in your path for a purpose.

One of my dearest friends is a Jewish man who lives in Jerusalem named Gideon Shor. Gideon is a tour guide par excellence. He has personally guided some of the most famous personalities in the world, including Hubert Humphrey, Norman Lear, many Catholic Cardinals, and numerous high-level government people. He is also good friends with the Kraft family, who owns the New England Patriots football team.

Through Gideon, I was introduced to Myra Kraft, a brilliant business woman and the wife of New England Patriots owner. Gideon continually told her that she should meet me. We spoke on the telephone several times, and I kidded her that I was going to "pray her team to the Super Bowl." That year, 2001, the team made it, and she sent me three tickets to the game in New Orleans! We attended the after-the-game gala, and late that night I met her for the first time.

She led me into the V.I.P. room to meet her husband and to take a picture of me with the Super Bowl championship trophy. The team repeated their Super Bowl appearance in 2003 in Houston, Texas. Myra again gave me two tickets, one for myself and one for Jonathan, to attend the number one sports event in the world. Both times the Patriots won the game—was it the prayer?

I did an exclusive telephone interview with her for TBN before the 2003 Super Bowl. It was a unique time for those who view Christian television to see and hear such a prominent business-woman. Our mutual love for Israel and the Hebrew nation links us as friends.

Through Myra's influence, doors opened for me to interview former Prime Minister Benjamin Netanyahu during a trip to Israel. "Bibi," as his close friends call him, said something that night that has remained in my spirit. He said, "Many of us Israelis have discovered that our true friends in America are not in the government, but the many Evangelical Christians who faithfully stand with Israel." He shared how, when traveling to America, it was common for Christians to speak to him and tell him they "love Israel and are praying for the people and the nation."

Gideon was instrumental in introducing me to many leading rabbis and spiritual leaders in the nation. In the mid-1980s, a major excavation, closed to the public, occurred in the Western Wall Tunnels. Through Gideon's relationship with Rabbi Yehudah Getz, Pam was one of the first women to enter this enclosure. For four years in a row, our group secretly entered the chambers at night, with the special permission of the rabbi.

I saw rooms and chambers that have since collapsed and may never be opened again. In 1988, with three others I toured the rubble that was the destruction of Jerusalem in 70 A.D. We saw bones of animals, and the fragile bones of humans who were slain during the historic siege of the city. It was awesome, and at the same time sad, to stand where so many people had met their death by the hands of the Roman legion.

In 1988, while standing in the tunnel with our tour group, I was informed by Rabbi Zvi that they knew the location of the Ark of the Covenant. He said it was about 70 meters from where we were standing. It is alleged that in 1981 a team was excavating the area and came across a number of water cisterns near an ancient gate. Rabbi Getz came to the scene and observed a crack in the "wall." He shined a flashlight in the small opening and saw a portion of the Ark.

Getz alleges that it was covered with old, dried animal skins, and the cherubim were damaged. Rabbi Getz told me on several occasions that he knew the hiding place of the lost Ark of the Covenant; this was also repeated by certain rabbis at the Temple Institute in Jerusalem. A book, *Return to Sodom and Gomorrah*, by Charles Pellegrino, states:

> Rabbis Shlomo Goren and Yehudah Getz insisted that during one of their explorations of the tunnel system they actually saw some of the lost Temple treasures, including the Ark of the Covenant, when they broke into a secret vault and pointed a flashlight through the opening. There were objects of wood and gold among the blocks of fallen stone rubble, and what appeared to be the lid of the Ark—crushed, but with one of its *keruvim* still intact. (*Return to Sodom and Gomorrah.* New York: Random House, 1994, p. 279.)

One of the most exciting moments came when a small group of friends rode with Gideon to the heart of the West Bank community of Samaria. The elevation was so high that the weather was spitting snow and sleet. We met one of the Samaritan priests who showed us an ancient scroll written in old Hebrew before the 6th century. That day, we learned that the Samaritans were excavating on the mountain of Gerizim. In their religious tradition, this is where Abraham offered Isaac.

Climbing the mountain, we came to fresh excavations exposing the ruins of the ancient Samaritan Temple, built after

Nehemiah expelled certain priests from the Temple in Jerusalem. This same site was the place the woman at the well mentioned when she stated, "Our fathers worshiped God in this mountain" (John 4:20). There we stood, on the very stones that once housed the Temple of the ancient Samaritans.

I will always be grateful to my friend, Gideon, for helping to fulfill the dreams of thousands of Americans who desire to tour the land of the Bible. Through our tours to Israel, I have gained valuable Hebraic and prophetic insight that I have shared in messages for many years.

THE PARTNERS OF THE MINISTRY

When Christ instructed Peter to launch out into the deep for a great catch of fish, Peter took his boat and his net. The haul of fish was so large that he immediately "beckoned to his partners" to bring their ships and enjoy the fruit of his labor (Luke 5:1-7). Many of the fish would have been lost without the assistance of Peter's fishing partners!

For years, our ministry did not have a Partner base, or a core group of people who prayed for and financially supported the ministry. When we began our cassette tape ministry, we also organized a "7 a Month Club" monthly tape club. The early members of the Tape Club were mostly a few relatives. Today it has grown to several thousand members who receive a recorded message each month. The income received, over and above the cost of the tape, is used to help print the *Voice of Evangelism* magazine.

The decision to not ask for funds in our monthly letters has many disadvantages. First, people often assume you have the income you need to accomplish your assignments, but this is seldom true. Secondly, without special letters informing people of the need or opportunity to give to a major project, we may cut our financial help in the process. For many years our product sales carried much of the financial load for the outreach ministry.

After prayer, the inspiration came to me to form a "Partner's Strike Force." These are the people who are blessed by our ministry, believe in our vision, and desire to support the ministry through monthly giving. As an added benefit, we give each partner a special password on our web site that takes them to a Partner section, with special messages, updates and information. This way we can better connect with those who are partners with us in this worldwide ministry. The partner base is growing each week. The ministry is hosting a partner conference each year and will be hosting more as the partner base grows.

Lessons I Have Learned from these Experiences

- ♦ Guard your friendships today because you may need those friends tomorrow.

- ♦ God connects people in life to be a blessing to one another.

- ♦ Some friends are temporary acquaintances, others are permanent friendships.

- ♦ The older you get, the more you will cherish your friends and love the memories you make.

- ♦ God uses people to help you meet those who will help open doors of opportunity for you.

- ♦ Protect your friend's integrity and reputation just as you would your own family's.

CHAPTER 14

A COMMITMENT FOR HANDLING FINANCES

Not slothful in business; fervent in spirit, serving the Lord (Romans 12:11).

A COMMITMENT FOR HANDLING FINANCES

Throughout the history of the Christian church, some men and women who were called and chosen for ministry have fallen into sins of the flesh, causing their ministries to slide to an immediate halt. Valuable messages were lost and precious souls were impacted by their failure.

It has been said that the three sins that have destroyed more men are sins of pride, illicit sex, and money. These three things become the three most dangerous pitfalls. They are the PMS (P-pride), M (money), S (sex). I have attempted to guard myself from these three snares.

Coming from a humble background, I am appreciative of God's blessing but I refuse to fall to pride. I realize that without the Holy Spirit's help, I could do nothing. I have been married to one woman since 1982. We are deeply in love and trust we will be raptured or grow old together. As for money, as a young man I determined to lay down certain principles concerning personal and ministry finance that I have kept to this day.

One reason money can become a snare is that most ministers enter the ministry with major shortages of the green stuff. The stories you hear or read, telling of how a young minister and his wife experienced lack, are often understated.

Years ago, Pam and I booked a revival meeting in Maine. We traveled three days, preached one week and traveled three days back to Cleveland. The offering was $500.00. This amount had to cover three weeks of living expense, including all the fuel, hotels and meals.

On another occasion, I preached for three weeks in South Carolina. The offerings were so low that we considered speaking to the bank and taking out a personal loan to help us pay the basic bills. Most local churches have members who tithe on a regular basis. They have faithful friends who support through weekly offerings.

As an evangelistic ministry, we have no guarantee that anyone is going to financially support what we do. We know how to abound and to be abased. Some months there is more than enough, and other months I have wondered who closed the windows of heaven! However, I have learned that God is always faithful.

THE OFFERINGS FOR THE MINISTRY

When we formed the Voice of Evangelism Outreach Ministries in 1984 as a nonprofit religious organization, three things happened immediately. First, all offerings, unless publicly designated, go entirely to the Voice of Evangelism and not to Pam or myself. We are on a monthly salary set by our board of directors. Offerings in the revivals and camp meetings, unless designated for other speakers, are used entirely for the ministry.

Secondly, everything connected to the ministry is owned by the ministry. The buildings, television equipment, office equipment—literally everything linked to V.O.E.—are owned by Voice of Evangelism and not by us personally. The assets cannot be given to us for personal use, only for use in the ministry. We own our own house which we are paying for. We own two personal vehicles, our clothes and the furniture in our house.

Thirdly, I have never taken any royalties from the books, tapes, CDs, DVDs, or videos I have produced. Although my voice is on every audio recording and I have personally written over 24 books, I have never received a royalty check from a book publisher, because the income is directed back into the ministry. There are certain benefits to having a nonprofit organization. They are:

♦ We can file for a special mailing permit, which saves the ministry money.

♦ We can file for tax exemption on many equipment purchases.

♦ We can give a tax deduction to people who donate to the ministry.

Personal Commitments to the Ministry

Many years ago, I made several personal commitments to the Lord concerning our ministry. When we began our mailing list for the V.O.E. magazine, *I made a commitment* that I would never sell the list of names to marketing groups. Large mailing lists are purchased on a continual basis by various companies, and can bring huge amounts of money. If you ever order something from a magazine, you will probably be on the "list" from that moment on, and be swamped with mail order magazines. I have never sold names and I never will.

The second commitment I made was not to send out monthly letters requesting funds for the ministry. As a teenager I remembered receiving donation appeals from ministries and noticed that they all looked the same. The stationary and envelope was printed on the same type of paper, with black ink and with important statements underlined with blue ink. Then I found out that most of the ministries were using the same company to do their fundraising letters! By not asking for funds I may have limited other ministry outreaches but God has honored us and allowed us to pay our ministry expenses without borrowing.

The third commitment I made involved the resource material. The books, tapes, videos, CDs, and DVDs contain messages that have impacted hundreds of thousands of people around the world. From about 1980 to this present time we have sold millions of dollars in resource material that has all gone back into the ministry. If we had chosen to receive a small royalty for just the books we could have been very wealthy. However, Pam and I decided and affirmed that our main treasures would be eternal treasures.

Personal Commitment to Our Personal Finances

Many people would find this hard to believe, but in the early 1990s, my yearly salary was $18,000 a year. Some said I could not live off of this amount. At that time, however, we traveled 250 to 300 days a year, staying in hotels and eating meals provided by churches. In the mid-1990s, our C.P.A. told me that as the ministry grew financially, the I.R.S. and major financial advisors said my salary must be representative of the income.

I refused a raise for three years, until the board members threatened to resign. I told them my heart was to put everything I could into the ministry. Because of their insistence, the salary was increased.

We operate our personal lives in the same manner as our ministry—debt-free when possible. Of course we have a house payment, but the contents are paid for. We try not to make a purchase unless it can be paid in full or unless the bank card can be paid without the interest charge. This relieves us of excessive financial pressure.

Pam and I both support the church with our tithes and offerings. She and I both pay tithes on everything we receive, including salaries and personal love gifts. We love to bless people we know and have always seen the Lord return the favors. Several times Pam has given away furniture, clothing and several automobiles. We have discovered we can receive a better blessing by sowing instead of selling!

Our many blessings are a reflection of our desire and commitment to be givers and not takers.

PERSONAL COMMITMENT TO OUR MARRIAGE

Marriage is an amazing relationship. A man and woman from two totally different backgrounds join in holy matrimony and unite their visions into one goal. God weaves their desires into a wonderful fabric and calls it a home.

Prior to marrying Pam, I was concerned that a companion in my life would interfere with my personal study and prayer time. A week before our marriage, I gave her a bold warning. I said, "You need to know this. Don't ever turn into a negative, complaining 'biddy.' If you become difficult to live with, I will fast and pray and the Lord will remove you!"

I remember that she looked at me with the same warmth she does today, and said, "Okay." We have laughed at that silly statement. She should have said, "And you need to know I won't live with a lazy man!" Pam is not a biddy and I am not lazy!

Prayer and study are priorities in my life. After marriage, Pam would join me in prayer. Our schedule was so hectic that she would often become tired in the middle of the day—during prayer time. On several occasions she would fall asleep as I was praying. I nicknamed her "Sister Peter," since Peter was known for sleeping during the prayer meetings! She prayed in a quiet fashion, but my occasional burst of "glory" or "hallelujah" would revive her from the twilight zone!

We both determined before we were married never to go to bed angry at one another. It would be sad if we were mad and one of us passed away during the night. The last memory would be that of an argument. We said we would apologize before going to bed. A few times I have apologized before preaching. I told her "There is no way I am going to get up there and try to minister after this fuss. Now forgive me."

Once she looked at me and didn't respond. She just wanted to see me sweat a bit. On another occasion I called her from a hotel after a meeting and said, "We're not going to bed even though I'm here and you're there. We are getting this thing straightened out right now."

God has given us two amazing children, Jonathan and Amanda. As the sands of time continues to pour through the hourglass, Pam and I have determined to spend more quality time with the children and with each other.

Personal Commitment to Our Children

Children are, without a doubt, the greatest joy in life. Jonathan is my "hanging buddy." We both enjoy just hanging out with each other, and he is a natural-born comedian. I wondered why Amanda was born later in my life, and then realized God must have given her to me to be a joy in my latter years and perhaps to take care of me and her mom as we get older. After all, when she is 18 years old, I will be 60.

Many ministers' children resent the ministry. Their father spends all his time with other people, traveling or constantly in meetings. Dad was once reflecting on our upbringing and said his biggest mistake was not spending more personal time with the children. In Dad's time, the concept among ministers was, "The ministry comes first, because God comes first." I have personally committed to spending time with my children every opportunity I can. They grow up fast and eventually the nest is empty and mom and dad are alone again.

Pam and I talk about "making memories." We suggest that people take a lot of pictures; keep a journal, if possible; and never miss an opportunity to spend time with those you love the most, especially your children.

LESSONS I HAVE LEARNED FROM THESE EXPERIENCES

- ◆ Make commitments early in life and stay with them, no matter what.

- ◆ People will respect someone who stays the course over many years.

- ◆ Your commitment to your family is more important than any other decision.

- ◆ Don't seek for money. Do God's will and money will be there to complete your work.

- ◆ Your children are more important than your job or your money.

CHAPTER 15

A VISION FOR THE FINAL HALF OF THE RACE

Where there is no vision, the people perish; but he that keepeth the law, happy is he (Proverbs 29:18).

A VISION FOR THE FINAL HALF OF THE RACE

The founder/director of our *Daughters of Rachel* intercessory ministry, Bea Ogle, approached me several years ago after experiencing a spiritual dream. She dreamed of seeing a large harvest field with ripe grain waving in the wind.

A small, hand sickle lay nearby. The Lord said, "This is the sickle I gave to Perry when he began his ministry."

She then observed a second sickle the size of a man. The Lord revealed, "This is the sickle he has been using." Then she saw a sickle so large that it was impossible for me to hold up without assistance. The Lord said, "This is the next sickle I am giving to Perry, but he will need assistance to help carry it!"

After this dream God opened the door for our program, Manna-Fest, on several large television networks. This move increased the volume of mail, emails and orders. I realized the harvest demanded laborers to help us carry the sickle. This "help" has come from our partners, friends in local churches, and the anointed prayer ministry of the *Daughters of Rachel.*

Every church, ministry and minister needs a strong prayer base of vigilant prayer warriors to continually intercede for their spiritual leaders. Fervent prayer is like preventive medicine—don't wait until you are sick to get help. Strong intercessors can pray away the powers of darkness and bind the possible attacks of the enemy to prevent disaster. There are over 1,000 women of prayer in our prayer ministry.

Men must also be trained in spiritual warfare. Robert "Bob" Gesing is founder and president of *Elijah's Mantle*, a men's ministry reaching out through the Voice of Evangelism. The *Men of the Mantle* is a fellowship of Christians from various denominations who link their faith and creative ideas together for the advancement of the kingdom of God. These special outreaches involve believers who help us carry the vision for global evangelism.

The Seven Point Outreach

For the first 25 years of our ministry, the Holy Spirit had us to emphasize a special Seven Point Outreach Plan. This plan was revealed to me at 18 years of age, while in deep prayer. These seven outreaches have been refined and updated since their origin, but remain the cornerstone and purpose for our ministry.

The Seven Point Outreach Plan
1. Revival meetings
2. Camp meetings and conventions
3. Overseas meetings and evangelistic thrusts
4. Printing the *Voice of Evangelism* magazine
5. Audio tape and videotape resource material
6. The Samaritan Fund outreach
7. The Manna-Fest telecast

As we enter the second phase of ministry, I believe the Holy Spirit has inspired me to focus on seven more major outreaches to impact the global harvest:

1. Expanding Manna-Fest

The weekly telecast, Manna-Fest with Perry Stone, will continue to be priority. The program airs throughout North America and on two major satellites that reach over 120 nations in the world. Our mission is to expand on as many networks as possible to reach the maximum number of viewers possible. There is a potential for millions of individuals to be reached by the messages on the weekly telecast.

2. Global Missions Department

Our ministry presently supports several international missionaries who are impacting their regions around the world. Our future plans are to form a strong Missions Department housed on the Voice of Evangelism ministry campus in Cleveland.

This department will serve as the nerve center for world missions outreaches, assisting missionaries, evangelistic soul-winning efforts, and the building of churches, orphanages and supporting foreign Bible schools.

3. Mentor Training Center

A future mentoring school, *The Manna Center*, will be built on the campus, and will enable us to bring together between 50 and 70 men and women at one time who are called into the ministry.

We will be able to train them a week out of each month in areas of ministry not commonly taught in Bible schools and Christian colleges. This time of impartation will be conducted in a future facility where the students can stay, be fed and attend the classes on location. During 11 months out of the year, 500 to 700 individuals can receive impartation and revelation for ministry.

4. Home Bible School

The enormous resource tools and spiritual knowledge acquired by Perry Stone in over 36,000 hours of study and during years of ministry will be compiled into a home Bible School curriculum. This *School of the Word* will be made available to any student who wishes to study at home at his own pace. This future outreach hopes to train thousands of individuals with the same knowledge and revelation God has given to us.

5. Overseas Evangelism

The Holy Spirit has promised us that we would reach the heathen in the nations of the world. We have seen this come to pass on a limited scale, having traveled to nine countries to preach evangelistic meetings during our ministry. We believe that in the future, the doors will open wide for an end-time harvest of souls in nations throughout the world.

6. Translation of Ministry Resource Materials

The majority of our books, tapes and videos are available only in the English language. Our vision is to translate these life-changing resource tools into as many languages as possible and distribute them throughout the world. This will be accomplished through the printed page and through special Internet sites.

7. Orphanages and Assisting the Needy

Voice of Evangelism presently supports several orphanages in foreign countries financially. Our future goal is to not only increase this support, but to establish orphanages of our own which can be supported by families and churches in North America.

The Lord has placed these seven outreaches in my spirit for the next half of my race. We will develop each outreach and expand only as God provides the funds, and guides the timing of each outreach. Our age indicates we are halfway through the race, but we are not finished yet!

CHAPTER 16

WHAT YOU WANTED TO ASK PERRY AND PAM

But I press on, that I may lay hold of that for which Christ Jesus has also laid hold of me (Philippians 3:12).

WHAT YOU WANTED TO ASK PERRY AND PAM

QUESTION: IF YOU COULD REDO ONE THING, WHAT WOULD YOU DO DIFFERENTLY?

Perry: There have been two—no, actually, three—things I wish I could do over.

Pam: And I know what one of the three is!

Perry: Okay. You tell me and I will see if you are right.

Pam: You and I were married on a Friday night in Northport, Alabama. We went out to Red Lobster with about 40 people for dinner, then spent the night at the Northport Holiday Inn. The following morning we traveled directly to a revival that continued for three straight weeks. You never took me on a honeymoon!

Perry: I confess you are right. That was the stupidest thing I ever did in my life. I was so spiritually minded I wasn't of much earthly good. I promise I will take you on a honeymoon one day!

Pam: Well, we have traveled quite a bit and enjoyed our time together. You've made up for it.

Perry: Now back to the things I would change if I could.

First of all, I would have stayed in contact with ministers who invited me to their church. The early meetings often continued for 3-11 weeks, and I canceled revivals quite often. This was not wise. I was traveling and had no office or personal secretary to help me keep in touch with pastors. Some invitations were lost in stacks of mail after several months.

Secondly, I have closed revivals down that I knew should have continued. One in particular could have gone on for many months, and we were invited to move it to a public school auditorium. I allowed other ministers to pressure me into closing the meeting, and I still think I missed the perfect will of God.

Thirdly, I would have married Pam sooner and had more children. I would like another one now.

Pam: Well, the marrying sooner is fine, but having more children is out of the question, unless you want to adopt one.

Perry: I would love to have another child, but Pam works so hard already I want her to enjoy me as she gets older! So, Pam, what would you do over if you could?

Pam: That's a difficult question because I believe we have followed the Lord. I think I would have had the children a little sooner. Handling a small child when you are over 40 is different than when you are 30.

QUESTION: WHAT IS THE HARDEST PART OF WHAT YOU DO?

Perry: I still enjoy traveling, but I confess that packing, unpacking and dragging the luggage around does get monotonous. I have been doing this nonstop, almost every weekend, since 1977. Since we purchased a small airplane and can return home after ministering, it helps to prevent travel burnout.

Pam: I would say the most difficult part is not having a steady eight-hour workday the way most people do. Our job seems to never end. For example, most of our workers work from Monday though Friday and are off on Saturday and Sunday. Perry will go to the office Monday through Friday and preach Saturday and Sunday, then be back in the office Monday through Friday. He often brings work home, spending hours planning or studying. People who work an 8 to 5 job don't realize how easy they have it compared to a minister who travels the nation!

Perry: That's true. I get amused at some well-meaning saint who says, "Preaching is an easy job." One minister heard a member make that statement and the preacher assigned the member to prepare a message and preach on Sunday morning. The member called the pastor late Saturday night and said, "I haven't slept all week. I am a nervous wreck. If you'll preach tomorrow, I'll keep my big mouth shut!" It's easy to criticize another man's work when you've never carried his burdens!

Pam: I want to say I am thankful that Perry has adjusted our schedule and is able to be at home more often than in the past. I remember when the revivals would continue every night for an average of three weeks. Now he does weekends and special meetings throughout the week. This enables him to be home with the family more often.

Perry: Part of the reason I am home more is that the emails, personal mail and television ministry require more of my time in the office. I have determined, however, that I am not going to try to win the world and let my children grow up without their father. Too many ministers live in regret of not watching their kids grow up and spending more time with them. If I win the whole world and spiritually lose my family, I feel I will have failed as a father.

Question: What do you enjoy most about each other?

Perry: This may sound silly, but the older I get I really enjoy snuggling up next to Pam at night when the children are asleep and it is very quiet. I also enjoy our lunchtime together. When I hear the car pull up behind my office, I really become excited to see Pam and Amanda coming to get me for lunch. I also enjoy just flirting with her. I have learned the simple things are often the most important and most enjoyable.

Pam: The thing I love most about Perry is I know he is a man of God. I consider it an honor to be the wife of a man who puts God first. I have always liked his hair. I even like the grey in it!

Perry: When I was single my hair was about the only thing going for me. One day I told the secretaries in the office that when I was single I was so homely looking that I couldn't get a date. I showed them an old picture and you should have heard the comments of "Eww" and "Gross" coming from them! I looked like a skeleton in a suit.

Pam: Your looks weren't that bad or I may not have been attracted. However, you have improved greatly over the past 23 years.

Question: What do you dislike most about each other?

Perry: I dislike the fact that she is right most of the time. At times she will give me important advice concerning a person or a situation. I will disagree and eventually she is proven right. It is just disgusting to see a woman who is not wrong that often (ha)!

Pam: I am married to a "workaholic." Perry is so consumed with the burden he carries that it is difficult for him to enjoy any free time. He is always "revelating." Often we will be eating and he will reach for a pen and paper to write down something he is receiving from the Lord. I understand it is all a part of the call, but it can be a challenge at times.

QUESTION: HAVE YOU EVER HAD ANY DIFFICULTY IN YOUR MARRIAGE?

Perry: I would not call it difficulty, but it was more of a season of misunderstanding. It happened after Jonathan was born. I was working at the office from 9 a.m. to 2 or 3 o'clock in the morning because we couldn't afford to hire more people.

Pam: I was dealing with a newborn, my first, and Perry was working from 9 to about midnight or longer. I felt he had a mistress and her name was "the ministry."

Perry: At the same time I went through a period of serious depression. I didn't want to read the Bible, pray, answer the mail or do anything involved in the ministry. I felt like I was drifting from the people I love the most, but I didn't know what to do.

Pam: That's when we were in a tent revival in Alabama and Perry told the people he was under an attack. That night they prayed for him and he felt something break in his spirit.

Perry: We also went on a cruise—away from the letters, the phones and people. It was a great move for us, and it gave us time we needed as a family. That's when I saw the importance of spending quality time with Pam and Jonathan (and now Amanda).

Pam: He has become mellower and less hyper. When I first saw him preach, it was like watching a tennis match. He would run to the left of the pulpit and run to the right. He would throw off his suit coat and sometimes take off his shoes.

Perry: Yes, yes, living with you has refined me!

Pam: It is true. Remember all those ties you collected? Before we were married? I gave away about 100 of the ugliest ties I had ever seen.

Perry: They were ugly to you but precious to me. Each one had a story behind it (ha)!

Pam: Well the stories ended up at the Salvation Army! And what about those shoes? He went to the North Cleveland Church of God and preached to 1,000 people wearing a pair of black shoes with black duct tape on the back of them! One of the older members of the church bought him a new pair of high-class leather shoes.

Perry: That's not the worst part. I had a black suit that I wore quite often. In fact, during a four-week revival in Pulaski, Virginia, the older women in the church requested to take my suits to the laundry. One woman, Birdie Viars, said, "So many people were falling out in the spirit in the services, we thought it might be the smell from the suits!" That is bad news when you are in a four-week revival. I would not let anyone but Mom do my laundry.

Pam: So the Lord gave me to you to be a helpmate, and you sure needed one to help you dress better and keep your clothes in good condition.

Perry: I don't disagree in the least, but I would love to have some of those ties today. They would be back in style!

Question: Everyone has a love language. Do you know yours?

Perry: I never understood this until Pam read a book on the five love languages. It did more to help me understand her and to understand why you must be careful around other women who will read into what you do as a love language, when you mean nothing by your actions.

Pam: It is a great book and I recommend it to every couple: *The Five Love Languages* by Gary Chapman.

Perry: I think my love language is probably affection and touch. I sometimes say it is the Italian DNA in me. I am a huggy-touchy type of person. Because of this, I must exercise more caution.

Sometimes I'll be talking to someone and just automatically be patting them on the back. With Pam I am always hugging her, or asking her to give me a kiss.

Pam: I have had to work on this because I am not, by nature, a very affectionate person. I express my love for my family by keeping the house clean and by cooking a good meal for them. However, I enjoy our family time more than anything else. For years I had to drag Perry out of the office or off the road just to enjoy a week's vacation. Now he enjoys hanging out with the kids, just being at home more, and we love our family time.

Perry: I have also recognized the fact that Pam's father was not in her life from age 12. A little girl often learns affection or how to love her husband from her father. Many wives struggle with certain things in their marriage because of how they were mistreated, abused or ignored by a father. One should never use this as an excuse of not being a good companion, however.

QUESTION: WHAT IS THE MOST REWARDING PART OF THE MINISTRY?

Perry: To me, seeing the spiritual results is the ultimate blessing of the ministry. Just as the apostle Paul felt, my greatest blessing is the fruit of the ministry. When I see a soul saved, a believer baptized in the Spirit or a sick body healed, then this is the reward of the ministry.

Pam: I agree with Perry, but will add something. I love the many people we have met and the friends we have made over the years. This is why we love camp meeting so much. It is a time when we get to be with many of our partners and closest friends. I believe our partners are the best people in the entire world.

Perry: There is no doubt about it. We have many people who have been involved over the years with other major ministries and they connect with our folks and say, "You have the best partners of any people we have ever met." They really love each other.

Another point to make is that I love to watch people grow spiritually. Several young men who are now full-time pastors and evangelists were saved under my ministry. There is no greater joy than to know we have spiritual sons in the ministry! It is both heart-warming and gratifying.

QUESTION: WHAT ARE YOUR PLANS FOR YOUR CHILDREN?

Perry: We adore the children. Pam and I have said that we want them to be what God has placed in their hearts. Jonathan is very intellectual and rational; he enjoys computers. Amanda seems to be interested in helping people. She always wants to help you in the house, pack the car, or do something.

Pam: Amanda loves watching programs that deal with hospitals, the sick, women having children, you know . . . the doctor programs. She has a strong sense of compassion.

Perry: It would be great to see both of my children involved in ministry in some form. To me, this would be more important than their becoming respected world leaders. I am praying for God's will in their lives, however.

QUESTION: HOW DO YOU BOTH DESIRE TO BE REMEMBERED?

Perry: We both know that only God can give us a long life, and no man is promised a guaranteed number of days. Considering mortality is something one must ponder. I have always said there are three things I hope can be said about me:

First, that I did all that the Lord commanded me to do

Secondly, that I was a good husband and a father. I would rather be known as a great father and husband than a great preacher. The public does not know you as intimately as your family. If your wife and children say you were the best, then that is the greatest compliment.

Thirdly, I want it to be said that I left a good name for my children. If, by the grace of God, I can impact my family, do God's perfect will, and leave a good name I will be happy when I depart.

Pam: I guess my wish is very simple. I want people to know that I was a person who cared about other people, and was never selfish with my blessings. I loved to share things with other people.

Perry often scolds me (in love) when I plan on cooking for a lot of people at the house. He gets concerned that I am wearing myself out or that I am taking on too much, but part of my joy in life is being a blessing to others.

Perry: This may not be the time to mention this, but the secretaries in the office often talk, when Pam is not present, about how giving and caring she is. I have heard them say on many occasions that they have never met anyone more giving.

Pam: I'm not doing it to be seen or even to be appreciated. . .

Perry: I know that. I realize that. However, others do see it. I have personally seen you give away our furniture, several vehicles, clothes and money to people in need. That's why I believe you are so blessed!

Pam: You are not a selfish person, either. You have always been a giver.

Perry: I know that it is "more blessed to give than to receive." That's why we teach our children to tithe and give. Jonathan has been tithing since he was three years old. We pay tithe on every birthday or Christmas gift the children receive.

QUESTION: WHAT DO YOU SEE IN THE FUTURE FOR YOURSELVES AND YOUR MINISTRY?

Perry: I want to continue in obedience to the will of God and expand our outreach ministry as God directs.

Pam: I don't ever think about where we are heading. I have confidence in Perry and his obedience to God. I just let the Lord open doors or direct us in His plan and His timing. Whatever He does is always a good thing.

Question: What is your ultimate goal?

Perry: I was once asked what was the one thing I wanted to be able to say when my earthly ministry is complete. Without hesitation I replied, "I want to be as Joshua was when he was concluding his earthly assignment. The Bible says, 'He left nothing undone of all that the Lord commanded' (Joshua 11:15). I want to be able to say that I completed every assignment and performed God's will for my life."

I have a desire to finish the race strong. In 1967, R.L. Rexrode died with cancer on a farm in the mountains of West Virginia. I saw him for the last time when I was eight years old. He died sick in body, but he finished his race in faith.

John Bava was a joy to those who knew him. When he lay dying in a hospital in Elkins, West Virginia, he could not move, speak or open his eyes. His body was lifeless, but when he breathed his final breath, his spirit crossed the finish line strong.

My Dad is over 71 now, and eventually he will step across the finish line and receive a marvelous reward for his faithfulness. His physical frame is thinner and his steps may be a little slower, but when the time comes to exit earth and enter the gates of glory, he will cross the threshold and hear the Master say, "Well done."

My desire and my prayer is that I will be able to finish strong. If the coming of the Lord tarries, perhaps I can pass the torch off to my son or my daughter, or a minister who can be mentored under my ministry. At this season I can say I have the vision, I have the strength and I can feel God's hand leading me.

I'm not finished yet. I've got my second wind and I am running the second half of my race to win the prize. My ultimate goal is to cross the finish line . . . and win the gold.

Pam: My ultimate goal in life may be somewhat different from my husband's. Of course I want to finish the race strong and hear the Lord say, "Well done." However, as a wife and mother there is another perspective to my purpose in this life.

My love and life is centered on my husband and my children. I am a family-oriented person. My love language is quality family time. There is nothing I enjoy more than the four of us getting together and just having a good time as a family. If I have an ultimate goal in this life, it is to be a great wife to my husband, a loving mother to my children and a faithful friend to those who call me friend.

I always want to be remembered as a person who really cared about people and who loved them. There is still much to do and a race to run and a prize to gain. We are not finished yet!

MINISTRY INFORMATION RESOURCE PAGE

We welcome you to contact our ministry for additional information or resource materials such as books, videos, DVDs, CDs, and other informative study tools. You may request a free product catalog by contacting us.

Voice of Evangelism Outreach Ministries
P.O. Box 3595
Cleveland, TN 37320
Phone: (423) 478-3456
Fax: (423) 478-1392
Monday through Friday, 9 am to 5 pm EST

www.perrystone.org

LEARN MORE ABOUT

♦ Becoming a partner with our ministry through the Partner Strike Force

♦ Joining our Monthly Message Club

♦ Our yearly conferences and main event camp meetings

♦ Receive information about our annual Holy Land Tour

OUR MINISTRY OPERATES ACCORDING TO PHILIPPIANS 4:19

"But my God shall supply all your need according to His riches in glory by Christ Jesus."

About the Author

Dr. Perry Stone Jr., international evangelist, is founder and director of the **Voice of Evangelism Outreach Ministries** in Cleveland, Tennessee.

Perry has a rich heritage as a fourth-generation minister of the gospel. He began preaching at age 16, continued his external studies through Lee University, and eventually earned a Bachelor of Theology degree from Covenant Life Christian College.

He has also received two honorary doctorates: one from Wesley Synod (Toledo, Ohio) and an honorary Doctor of Philosophy in Christian Science from Saint Thomas-a-Becket Episcopal Synod in Canterbury, England.

The **Voice of Evangelism** has many branches of outreach, including a Seven Point Outreach for Global Evangelism. Reverend Stone writes and publishes a bi-monthly magazine, and has written and published many books, including three best sellers. He has produced an extensive library of teaching materials and videos on a wide variety of subjects.

He hosts the weekly television program, **Manna-fest,** which is aired nationwide on Christian TV stations and on satellite.

Perry resides in Cleveland, Tennessee, with his wife, Pam, and their two children.